GREAT BEERS

450 OF THE BEST FROM AROUND THE WORLD

Based on content previously published in DK's *The Beer Book*

EDITOR-IN-CHIEF **TIM HAMPSON**

METRO BOOKS
New York

METRO BOOKS
New York

An Imprint of Sterling Publishing
1166 Avenue of the Americas
New York, NY 10036

METRO BOOKS and the distinctive Metro Books logo
are trademarks of Sterling Publishing Co., Inc.

Project Editor Robert Sharman, Elizabeth Yeates
Project Art Editor Nihal Yesil
Designer Elma Aquino
Managing Editor Dawn Henderson
Managing Art Editors Christine Keilty, Marianne Markham
US Editors Jenny Siklós, Shannon Beatty
DTP Designers Harish Aggarwal, Pushpak Tyagi
DTP Manager Sunil Sharma
Production Manager, DK India Pankaj Sharma
Editorial Manager, DK India Glenda Fernandes
Senior Jacket Designer Nicola Powling
Pre-Production Producer Rebecca Fallowfield
Producer Kathleen McNally
Special Sales Creative Project Manager Alison Donovan

First American edition 2015
Published in the United States by DK Publishing
345 Hudson Street, New York, New York 10014
A Penguin Random House Company

Material previously published by DK in Great Beers (2008)

ISBN 978-1-4351-6055-2

A catalog record for this book is available from
the Library of Congress

Color reproduction by Colourscan
Printed and bound in China

001-284739-Aug/2015

2 4 6 8 10 9 7 5 3 1

www.sterlingpublishing.com

Contents

Introduction

This book is an adventure—a journey through a fascinating world of flavors, colors, and aromas. These pages constitute a trip around the world in 450 ales, porters, and pilsners, and an introduction to the master brewers behind the world's greatest drink.

These are exciting times for beer lovers. With the US leading the way in terms of innovation, in the last few decades brewers have been pushing at boundaries as never before. From Alaska to the Mexican border, America's craft brewers are brewing darker beers, bitterer beers, and hoppier beers than can be found anywhere else in the world. European beer styles are being taken apart and put back together with barely a nod to tradition. In brewing terms, there are simply no rules anymore.

Meanwhile, the great brewing nations of Europe—Germany, Belgium, the Czech Republic—still stand tall, with glorious tradition standing alongside intriguing innovation. Countries historically associated more with grape than grain are also making great strides—Italy's brewers are among the most experimental and ambitious worldwide, and their efforts have been yielding remarkable results.

The other good news for lovers of great beer is that it has never been easier for drinkers to sample such a wide range of beers from around the world. A trip to your local shop or supermarket will in most cases provide a selection of several of the brews featured in this book. More ambitious readers may be encouraged to travel further to track down exciting tipples and experience the brewing and drinking culture of some of the world's top beer destinations. If this appeals to you, this book introduces tours of Oregon, Brussels, the Cotswolds, Prague, and Bamberg—range of destinations representing the best of the old and new worlds of beer.

This book is intended for people who want to broaden their knowledge of beer and hunt down exciting brews from around the globe. It should encourage you never to ask just for a beer without first considering its style—pilsner or wheat, fruit or an American IPA, Belgian ale or a gueuze? For there can be few better pleasures—when returning home after a long day at work or just sitting in a favorite bar—than the pleasure of a great beer. But which one? The choice is yours—enjoy the experience.

Tim Hampson

Aass Bryggeri

Postboks 1530,
N-3007 Drammen, **NORWAY**
www.aass.no

Norway's oldest brewery dates
back to 1834. Named after Poul
Lauritz Aass (pronounced
"ouse"), it is a family-owned
business run by four generations
since 1860.

BREWING SECRET Aass brews
according to the strict 1516 Bavarian Law
of Purity, drawing its water from
the nearby lake of Glitre.

Aass Bock
DUNKLER BOCK **6.5%** ABV
Smooth and creamy; brewed using
Munich malt and Hallertau hops.
Lagered for at least three months.

Aass Juleøl
DUNKLER BOCK **6.2%** ABV
The most sought-after Christmas beer
in Scandinavia. Thick and malty with
a smooth, rich flavor.

Abbaye des Rocs

37, Chaussée Brunehault, B7387
Montignies-sur-Roc, **BELGIUM**
www.abbaye-des-rocs.com

Jean-Pierre Eloir, a former exciseman, took up brewing in 1979. The business has since expanded, with the beers gaining a good reputation, particularly abroad, and some are now being developed with export in mind.

BREWING SECRET Core beers are true to the spiced and well-bodied Walloon style; keg beers are often unfiltered.

Blanche des Honnelles
WITBIER **6**% ABV
Not your usual wheat beer, this one is made from malted barley, malted wheat, and home-malted oats.

Abbaye des Rocs Brune
BELGIAN DARK STRONG ALE **9**% ABV
Very spiced and sustaining, with a nourishing touch. Well-liked in Anglo-Saxon countries.

Adnams

Southwold, Suffolk, IP18 6JW
ENGLAND
www.adnams.co.uk

Its "Beers from the Coast" have been brewed in the classic English seaside town of Southwold since 1872. In recent years, technological innovation has driven refurbishment, while an emphasis on traditional methods has been studiously maintained. An eco-friendly distribution center—complete with living grass roof—summarizes the dynamic approach.

Adnams Broadsidee
STRONG BITTER **4.7**% ABV
Rich, fruitcake aromas dominate initially, giving way to an elegant hop and malt association.

Adnams Bitter
BITTER **3.7**% ABV
Aromatic hop and biscuit malt fragrances introduce a lingering, dry, and refreshingly bitter flavor.

Airbräu

Münchner Airportcenter,
Terminalstr. Mitte 18, 85356
München, **GERMANY**
www.allresto.de

This brewery has a unique
location: set between the two
terminals of Munich airport.
It opened in 2004 at the same
time as the airport's new
Terminal 2, and it includes a
much-frequented restaurant and
beer garden. Two brewing kettles
are situated right in the middle of
the restaurant.

Fliegerquell
LAGER 5.2% ABV
Deep golden, finely structured,
and classically dry. It is brewed
for international palates.

Kumulus
WHITE BEER 5.4% ABV
Typical yellow color; a sparkling,
very fresh white beer, refreshing
and full-bodied.

Aktien

Hohe Buchleute 3, 87600
Kaufbeuren, **GERMANY**
www.aktienbrauerei.de

The origins of brewing at the
Aktien brewery in Kaufbeuren
can be traced back to the early
14th century. In more recent
times, Aktien has taken over the
Löwen and Rosen breweries.

BREWING SECRET Aktien still brews its
beer strictly according to the Bavarian
Purity Law set in 1516.

Naturtrübes Kellerbier
KELLERBIER 5.1% ABV
Unfiltered and naturally cloudy
out of the cellar. The slightly sweet taste
is typical of one of the oldest styles of beer
in Bavaria.

Fendt Dieselrossöl
MÄRZEN 5.9% ABV
A malty, aromatic structure and
a full-bodied, slightly bitter taste.
Goes well with venison dishes.

Alaskan

5429 Shaune Drive
Juneau, AK 99801, **USA**
www.alaskanbeer.com

Although it is located in a coastal Alaska community cut off from the lower 48, Alaskan Brewing has grown into a force that spreads from the western coast of Canada down through much of the US west of the Rockies. Founders Geoff and Marcy Larson focused on native ingredients and recipes from the outset. Alaskan's first and flagship brew, Amber Ale, is based on a beer made across the channel from Juneau back at the turn of the 20th century.

Amber

ALTBIER 5% ABV
Clean caramel on the nose, brightened by spicy hops. Smooth and malty, with balanced bitterness.

Barley Wine Ale

BARLEY WINE 10.4% ABV
Cellared in a former gold mine. Rich and smooth, with dark caramel, cherries, and plums. Nicely balanced.

A. Le Coq

Tähtvere 56/62,
50050 Tartu, **ESTONIA**
www.alecoq.ee/en

This brewery was founded in
1826, and purchased in 1913
by A. Le Coq, a London-based
company. At the time, it was
looking for a brewery in the
Russian Empire where it could
produce its Imperial Stout rather
than export it from England.
Production was halted in the
1960s but revived in 1999.
A small museum is housed
in the former maltings.

Le Coq Porter
PORTER 6.5% ABV
A strong, dark beer—a worthy
successor to the famous Imperial
Extra Double Stout.

Double Bock
BOCK 8% ABV
A strong and warming light bock,
it has a surprisingly mellow finish
for a beer of this strength.

Alesmith

9368 Cabot Drive
San Diego, CA 92126, **USA**
www.alesmith.com

One of several San Diego
breweries that has pushed
Southern California to the
forefront of national brewing.
It has a wide following for its
mostly strong and often esoteric
beers, many barrel-aged and
vintage-dated.

BREWING SECRET Every employee
is an award-winning home brewer.

Speedway Stout
IMPERIAL STOUT 12% ABV
It's coffee-infused, complementing
a broad imperial palate of chocolate,
toffee, currants, and oily nuts.

IPA
INDIA PALE ALE 7.3% ABV
Brimming with hops and fruit salad
aromas, including notes of ripe mango
and pineapple.

Alhambra

Avenida de Murcia 1,
18012 Granada, **SPAIN**
www.cervezasalhambra.com

The Alhambra group was founded in 1925 and is named after Granada's famed Moorish palace. Spain's purest water comes from the nearby Sierra Nevada mountain range, and is used in the making of Alhambra beers.

BREWING SECRET The brewery uses traditional techniques that include fermentation lasting up to 39 days.

Alhambra Premium
LAGER 4.6% ABV

A soft gold in color, its nose is lemony and fresh with a hint of malt. A well-balanced, quaffable beer.

Mezquita
WHEAT BEER 7.2% ABV

A full-bodied, assertive red wheat beer with caramel notes and hints of pepper in the aroma.

Allagash

100 Industrial Way
Portland, ME 04103, **USA**
www.allagash.com

Focusing on Belgian-inspired beers, Allagash draws on tradition but does not shy away from innovation. In 2007 it became the first American brewery to build a traditional "coolship" (a huge, open, shallow pan) for spontaneous fermentation by wild yeasts.

BREWING SECRET Some specialty beers are aged in oak bourbon barrels.

Allagash White
WITBIER **6.2%** ABV
Appropriately cloudy, fruity, and refreshing. Brightened by subtle coriander and Curaçao orange peel.

Curieux
TRIPLE **10%** ABV
Allagash Tripel ale, aged in Jim Beam barrels. Orchard fruits and honey meet bourbon, vanilla, and wood.

Allersheim

Allersheim 6, 37603 Holzminden,
GERMANY
www.brauerei-allersheim.de

Founded in 1854, this brewery was, for Otto Baumgarten, merely a sideline to farming. He harvested the grain in his own fields, but had to buy in the hops. Production grew over the years, though, and today the brewery has 40 employees.

BREWING SECRET The beers are brewed to suit discerning local palates.

Landbier
PILSNER 5% ABV
A pilsner with a mash bill from light and dark malt. Soft in taste, with a typical malty aroma.

Blue Moon
BEER AND COLA 1.9% ABV
A pleasant mix of dry hops and cola. It's not too sweet, because the mix is produced without sugar.

Almond 22

Via Dietro le Mura 36/38,
65010 Spoltore (PE), **ITALY**
www.birraalmond.com

This microbrewery was founded
in 2003, in the seaside town of
Pescara, by Swedish-Italian Jurij
Ferri. He brews highly praised
ales inspired by British and
Belgian styles, as well as some
original, experimental beers that
use local ingredients.

Torbata

BARLEY WINE 8.7% ABV
Peated ale with a smoky flavor similar
to a Scotch whisky. Easy to drink despite
its strength.

Farrotta

SPELT WHEAT ALE 5.7% ABV
Cloudy golden ale brewed using
barley and locally grown spelt; easy-
drinking and thirst-quenching.

Amber

Bielkówko, ul. Gregorkiewicza 1,
83-050 Kolbud, **POLAND**
www.browar-amber.pl

Owned by the Przybylo family,
this medium-sized brewery is one
of the most modern in Poland.
Situated close to Gdansk in
Pomerania, an area with a rich
brewing tradition, the brewery
is a supporter of the Slow Food
movement, and organizes the
Kozlaki Bielkowskie food and
drink festival every September.

Koźlak

DUNKEL BOCK **6.5**% ABV
A ruby-red beer, it is rich in malt and
yeasty flavors, with a warming aftertaste.

Zywe

PILSNER **6.2**% ABV
Pale in color, it has lemon flavors
and uses hops and barley from the
Lubin region.

Amsterdam Brewing

21 Bathurst Street, Toronto,
Ontario, M5V 2NG, **CANADA**
www.amsterdambeer.com

Purity, passion, and revelry are
the watchwords for Toronto's first
brewpub. Founded in 1986, it was
an immediate success. Business
was brisk, and it soon moved to
another site before finding its
current home in 2005. The brewery
stands opposite the historic Fort
York, the 1793 birthplace of
modern Toronto. In 2003, when
the Kawartha Lakes Brewing
Company closed, its brands were
sold to Amsterdam Brewing.

KLB Nut Brown Ale
BROWN ALE 5% ABV
The unmistakable tang of East Kent
Golding hops. Sweet to taste, it has hints
of honey and chocolate.

Amsterdam Wheat Beer
WHEAT BEER 4% ABV
Light in color, with malt sweetness and a
hint of fresh bread. Often served chilled
with a slice of lemon.

Anchor

705 Mariposa St.
San Francisco, CA 94107, **USA**
www.anchorbrewing.com

Fritz Maytag saved Anchor
Brewing from closing in 1965,
introduced US drinkers to many
classic styles, and launched a
microbrewery revolution.

BREWING SECRET Maytag is known for
preserving the indigenous "steam style,"
which involves using bottom-fermenting
yeast at high temperatures in wide,
shallow, open pans.

Liberty Ale
PALE ALE 6% ABV
A benchmark American pale ale. Fruity
and floral on the nose; crisp bitterness
on the palate.

Anchor Steam
STEAM BEER 4.9% ABV
A signature woody, minty nose.
Well-rounded caramel flavors yield
to a firm, crisp finish.

Andechs

Kloster Andechs, Bergstr. 2,
82346 Andechs, **GERMANY**
www.andechs.de

The Benedictine monks of
Andechs began to produce beer
in 1455. The monastery updated
its brewery in 1972, investing in
modern equipment. Still closely
associated with the holy
mountain pilgrimage site
southwest of Munich, Andechs
today is a brand name that's
internationally known.

Bergbock Hell

BOCK 7% ABV

A strong beer, but it tastes mild and
aromatic. Its typical light sweetness
gives it a full body.

Doppelbock Dunkel

BOCK 7% ABV

This world-famous beer has a really
strong taste. The dark malts give it an
unmistakable character, with a light
aroma of hops in the finish.

Anderson Valley

17700 Highway 253
Boonville, CA 95415, **USA**
www.avbc.com

Set in Mendocino County's picturesque Anderson Valley, this solar-powered brewery mixes local and international styles and techniques. Some beer names are those of local landmarks, others are in Boontling, a regional dialect.

BREWING SECRET The copper brew kettles were rescued from a closed-down German brewery.

Boont ESB

EXTRA SPECIAL BITTER **6.8%** ABV
Citrussy hops layer fruit on top of bready malt. Tangy in the middle; a long and mildly bitter finish.

Barney Flats Oatmeal Stout

OATMEAL STOUT **5.7%** ABV
Impression of coffee and cream, sweetness balanced by roasted grains, the complexity heightened by earthy undertones.

Anheuser-Busch

One Busch Plaza
St. Louis, MO 63119, **USA**
www.anheuser-busch.com

Anheuser-Busch brews half the
beer sold in the United States,
including Budweiser and Bud
Light, two of the world's best-
selling brands. With its Michelob
line, seasonal specialties,
and beers produced by its
regional breweries for local
consumers, the company has
significantly broadened the
range of its beers.

Michelob

MALT LAGER 5% ABV
Returned to its all-malt roots in 2007.
Delicate, with a spicy nose, clean malt
middle and crisp, dry finish.

Stone Mill Organic Pale Ale

PALE ALE 5.5% ABV
Organic beer under the Green Valley
Brewing label. This ale is lightly bready
with earthy hop character.

Antares

17 Esquina 71, La Plata - P de Bs As, 7600, **ARGENTINA**
www.cervezaantares.com.ar

Antares is the brightest star in the Scorpius constellation, and the brewpub that shares its name sparkles too. Stylish and smart, it offers a lively alternative to beers from international brewers. Brews include a kölsch, a Scotch ale, a honey beer, a cream stout, a barley wine, and an imperial stout, with some variations in style.

Antares Stout Imperial

IMPERIAL STOUT 8.5% ABV
Intense liquorice and toasted flavors give way to roasted coffee and caramelized orange intensities.

Antares Kölsch

KÖLSCH 5% ABV
A well hopped and highly drinkable ale style. Good fruity overtones make it an ideal partner to food.

Apatinska Pivara

Trg Oslobodenja 5, Apatin,
25260 **SERBIA**
www.inbev.com

The biggest brewer in Serbia
and the largest in the Balkans,
this InBev-owned company
now has 46 percent of the local
market. The town of Apatini,
which is on the Danube, is in
a fertile barley-growing area
called Vojvodina. Records show
that brewing has taken place
in the town since 1756.

Jelen Pivo

LAGER 5% ABV
Light yellow in color, with a white,
wispy head. It has hints of grass and
grain and aromas of hops and malt.
Jelen means "deer."

Apatinsko Pivo

LAGER 5% ABV
A fresh-tasting beer with floral notes
and a citrus aroma.

Asia Pacific Breweries

459 Jalan Ahmad Ibrahim,
639934 **SINGAPORE**
www.tigerbeer.com

Widely available across Asia, AP's beers are now brewed in seven different countries. Tiger Beer—its most famous—was first produced in the 1930s, when the "Time for a Tiger" slogan was first used. Anthony Burgess named the first novel in his The Long Day Wanes trilogy *Time for a Tiger*.

Tiger
LAGER 5% ABV
A golden colored refreshing lager. It is normally served so chilled that its taste and aromas are masked.

ABC Extra Stout
STOUT 8% ABV
A strong but easy-drinking beer. The nose is robust, with roasted coffee and chocolate flavors.

Auer

Münchner Str. 80, 83022 Rosenheim,
GERMANY
www.auerbraeu.de

Between 1887 and 1920, Johann
Auer acquired several plots
of land and some breweries
around the town of Rosenheim,
southeast of Munich. Since
then, the company has
expanded considerably.

BREWING SECRET When it was
founded, this was one of the most
modern breweries in Bavaria.

Bajuware Dunkel
DUNKEL 5.5% ABV
Brewed in old-fashioned Bavarian
style, this beer has a malty aroma
and a full-bodied character.

Weizenbock
WHEAT BOCK 7% ABV
A strong, spicy specialty. A good
accompaniment to hearty cheeses
or sweet desserts.

Augustiner

Landsberger Str. 31-35, 80339
München, **GERMANY**
www.augustiner-braeu.de

Founded in 1328, this is the
oldest brewery in Munich and
one of only two in the city (along
with Hofbräu München) that do
not belong to a giant of the global
brewing industry. The site as it
is today was constructed in 1885.
Augustiner beer has become
famous around the world even
though the brewery does not
advertise itself.

Edelstoff

EXPORT **5.6**% ABV

The unusual dark golden color displays
its special character. A sweet and
obvious hop taste guides you to a
very malty finish.

Weissbier

WHEAT BEER **5.4**% ABV

Golden and cloudy, this is a full-bodied
wheat beer with a citrus taste and light
bitters in the finish.

August Schell

1860 Schell Road
New Ulm, MN 56073, **USA**
www.schellsbrewery.com

Family-owned since August
Schell founded it in 1860, this
brewery has perhaps the most
beautiful setting in the US, with
ornamental gardens and a former
carriage house converted into a
museum. In 2002 the company
took over production of the
legendary Grain Belt Premium
beer, when that brewery failed,
to save a Minnesota icon
from extinction.

Caramel Bock

BOCK **5.6%** ABV
Rich caramel on the nose, turning
rummy on the palate. Sweetness
lingers after a not-quite dry finish.

Schmaltz Alt

ALTBIER 5% ABV
Subtle combination of biscuit and
chocolate balanced by mild, slightly
spicy hop flavors and bitterness.

Au in der Hallertau

Schlossbrauerei Au in der Hallertau, Schlossbräugasse 2, 84072 Au, **GERMANY**
www.auer-bier.de

Au is at the heart of the largest hop-growing area in the world. It was linked with the master brewer Schweiger in 1590 and, since 1846, has been owned by six generations of the Earls Beck of Peccoz. A modern approach is an essential feature of the management at Au in der Hallertau.

Hopfengold
EXPORT 5% ABV
Golden color, full-bodied taste with fine bitters of hops and clear malt. Nice finish, not too sweet.

Holledauer Leichtes
WHEAT BEER 3.3% ABV
A cloudy yellow, light wheat beer, fresh and lightly sparkling; not too heavy a taste, and with a slightly bitter finish.

Avery

5763 Arapahoe Avenue
Boulder, CO 80803, **USA**
www.averybrewing.com

Located near the Rocky
Mountains, though in a
nondescript industrial park,
this brewery has earned a
reputation for its hoppy beers
and its astonishingly strong
beers (sometimes they are both).
These include a threesome
nicknamed the "Demons of Ale,"
in which the beers average
15 percent ABV apiece.

India Pale Ale

INDIA PALE ALE **6.3**% ABV
Piney, oily nose, with grapefruit and
orange from the aroma to the palate.
Unapologetically bitter.

Salvation

BELGIAN STRONG GOLDEN ALE **9**% ABV
Fleshy fruits, particularly apricots,
mingle with sweet, spicy aromas and
flavors, and a surprising hint of honey.

Le Baladin

Piazza V Luglio 15,
12060 Piozzo (CN), **ITALY**
www.birreria.com

Charismatic, pioneering Teo
Musso is internationally
known as one of the most
creative brewers in the world.
He has turned beer into a type of
wine and created beer truffles—
not even he knows what he will
do next.

BREWING SECRET Musso plays music
to his yeasts during the fermentation
process, believing that they respond.

Xyauyù
BARLEY WINE 12% ABV
Radical oxidization gives "solera"
sherrylike favors. A flat, warming,
velvety nightcap. A masterpiece.

Nora
SPICED ALE 6.8% ABV
Inspired by ancient Egypt, using
kamut grains, ginger, and myrrh.
A balsamic bitterness comes from
Ethiopian resins.

Baltika

6 Proezd, Parnas 4,
St. Petersburg, **RUSSIA**
www.eng.baltika.ru

The Russian beer market has been going through a period of rapid change as it continues to adjust to a capitalist economy. Baltika's rise has been swift, and it is now the country's largest beer producer. It brews the top two brands—Baltika and Arsenalnoye. The company accounts for more than seven out of ten beer sales, and exports to 46 countries.

Baltika No.3 Classic
LAGER 4.8% ABV
A malty nose gives way to a bitter finish. Widely available across Russia.

Baltika No.6 Porter
PORTER 7% ABV
A well-balanced beer. Dark roasted malts, chocolate and molasses flavors fill the glass, overlayed by a good hop finish.

Barley

Via C. Colombo, 09040 Maracalagonis
(CA), Sardinia, **ITALY**
www.barley.it

Skilful home brewer Nicola Perra
established this microbrewery in
2006 in southern Sardinia,
challenging the mass-market
lagers so popular in the region
(consumption here is the highest
in Italy).

BREWING SECRET Local ingredients
such as Sardinian wine wort and organic
honey are used in the ales.

Toccadibò
GOLDEN STRONG ALE **8.4%** ABV
A warming ale; spicy, hoppy and dry,
with intriguing bitter-almond notes
of amaretto.

BB 10
BARLEY WINE **10%** ABV
A unique brew made with *sapa*, the boiled
wort of local Cannonau grapes. A highly
distinctive nightcap.

Barons

1 Moncur Street, Woollahra,
New South Wales 2025, **AUSTRALIA**
www.baronsbrewing.com

"Beer barons" by name and
nature, this relative newcomer
has its brands produced under
contract and is one of the
country's fastest-growing craft
beer players; they are also
eyeing export markets in the
US and Russia.

BREWING SECRET Barons makes use
of indigenous "bush tucker" ingredients,
such as wattle seed and lemon myrtle.

Lemon Myrtle Witbier

BELGIAN WITBIER 5% ABV
Moderate carbonation, lime-scented
mid-palate with spicy hints, followed
by a clean, crisp finish.

Black Wattle Original Ale

SPICED AMBER ALE 5.8% ABV
Creamy mouthfeel, malt-driven, with
hints of roasted nuts, chocolate, and
milky coffee.

Bateman

Wainfleet, Lincolnshire,
PE24 4JE **ENGLAND**
www.bateman.co.uk

One of the country's oldest
and most picturesque family
breweries—with a windmill
towering high above—it has
a well-deserved reputation for
"good honest ales." A family
split almost destroyed the
business in the 1980s, but it
survived, blossomed, and has
developed a new brewhouse
and engaging visitor center.

XXXB

STRONG BITTER **4.8**% ABV
Classic russet-tan ale, with a well
constructed blend of malt, hops,
and fruitiness.

XB Bitter

BITTER **3.7**% ABV
Finely balanced, with an apple-influenced
hop aroma that lingers alongside the
malty flavor.

Bath Ales

Warmley, Bristol,
BS30 8XN **ENGLAND**
www.bathales.com

The founders' brewing backgrounds and insistence on traditional methods operating alongside cutting-edge technology has resulted in Bath Ale's reputation for distinctive, characterful, and flavorsome ales. The success of the business has led to the brewery twice outgrowing its premises since it was established in 1995. A bottling plant and shop continue the growth.

Gem Bitter
BEST BITTER 4.1% ABV
Rich and full-textured, with a malt, fruit, and bitter-sweet hop quality throughout.

Special Pale Ale (SPA)
PALE ALE 3.7% ABV
A prominent hop aroma and bitter malty touch complement its light-bodied character.

Bayern Meister Bier

1254-1 Kawaharabata,
Inouede-aza, Fujinomiya City,
Shizuoka 418-0103, **JAPAN**
www.bmbier.com

Brewmaster Stefan Rager
originally came to Japan to
brew at several start-up
microbreweries which opened
after the 1995 liberalization.
Later, with his Japanese wife,
he founded a boutique-style
brewery on the southern face
of Mount Fuji, dedicated to
German beer styles. The German
Embassy in Tokyo is one of his
most loyal customers.

Prinz Pils

PILSNER 5.5% ABV
Pale yellow, soft mouthfeel with low
carbonation. The subtle flavors are
in excellent balance.

Amadeus Doppelbock

DOPPELBOCK 8% ABV
Very deep reddish brown, with coffee,
toffee, and caramel aromas. Rich tangy
malt and high alcohol suggest rum-
soaked fruitcake.

Bear Republic

345 Healdsburg Avenue
Healdsburg, CA 95448, **USA**
www.bearrepublic.com

With a brewpub located amidst the Sonoma County wine-tasting rooms and a brewery north of town, Bear Republic presents a decidedly different break for wine tourists. Founding brewmaster (and fireman and race-car-driver) Richard Norgrove is just as skilled as any wine blender when merging hops flavors and aromas.

Racer 5
INDIA PALE ALE 7% ABV
Delightfully fresh grapefruit and thick piney aromas, built on a resinous, malty-sweet middle.

Hop Rod Rye
IMPERIAL INDIA PALE ALE 8% ABV
Bright, citrussy nose with spicy alcohols. A subtle blend of biscuit and clean rye. Incessant hops.

Beba

Viale Italia 11,
10069 Villar Perosa (TO), **ITALY**
www.birrabeba.it

Pioneering brothers Alessandro
and Enrico Borio brew a wide
range of regular and seasonal
lagers at their microbrewery
founded in 1996 near Turin. The
adjoining tap-room serves all the
house beers on draft along with
excellent food. The local specialty
is *gofri*, a crisp unleavened bread
stuffed with cheeses, cured
meats, or preserves.

Motor Oil

STRONG DARK LAGER 8% ABV

Ebony-colored, with strong notes of
liquorice and roasted coffee, beans
and a long, bitter finish. As viscous
as its namesake.

Talco

RYE LAGER 4.2% ABV

Seasonal "rye weizen-lager" is a
thirst-quenching treat on a hot
summer afternoon.

Bell's

8938 Krum Avenue
Galesburg, MI 49053, **USA**
www.bellsbeer.com

The oldest surviving microbrewery east of Colorado, Bell's (formerly Kalamazoo Brewing) has grown nearly 700-fold since its first sales in 1985. Bell's has built a new brewing facility outside Kalamazoo, but the original brewery remains, along with its appropriately named Eccentric Café. Bell's beers are famous for their intensity, although the brewery flagship is wheat-based.

Expedition Stout

IMPERIAL STOUT 11.5% ABV
Begins with an intense blast of dark fruit (figs and plums) that turns into chocolate, roasted coffee, and port.

Oberon Ale

WHEAT BEER 5.8% ABV
A summer refresher. Zesty, with orange rind in the aroma, and delicate spiciness behind that. A crisp, sharp finish.

Bere Romania

Str. Manastur Nr. 2-6,
Cluj Napoca, **ROMANIA**
www.sabmiller.com

Now a subsidiary of SABMiller, this brewery first opened in 1878. Its main brand, Ursus, is advertised under the slogan "The King of Romanian Beers." Each September the town of Cluj Napoca, in the heart of Transylvania, hosts a beer festival.

BREWING SECRET These beers are fermented using Bavarian yeast.

Ursus Premium Pils
PILSNER 5.2% ABV
Lively carbonation, a malty aroma, hints of fresh hops and bread, and lemony notes in the finish.

Timisoreana
LAGER 5% ABV
A light yellow, easy-drinking beer that doesn't challenge the senses. Made to a recipe from 1718.

Berg

Berg Brauerei Ulrich Zimmermann,
Brauhausstr. 2, 89548 Ehingen-Berg,
GERMANY
www.bergbier.de

Berg, founded in 1757, is family-
owned and one of the smallest
breweries in Germany.

BREWING SECRET Berg makes use
of corn in brewing, which is supplied
by an organic farm nearby.

Berg Original
LAGER **4.8**% ABV
Its smooth, dry taste makes this
beer the most popular brand offered
by the brewery.

Berg Märzen
MÄRZEN **6.1**% ABV
A typical strong beer. The taste is very
hearty, not least because of its high
dose of hops.

Bergquell

Weststr. 7, Löbau, **GERMANY**
www.bergquell-loebau.de

With its long brewing tradition, the Bergquell Brauerei Löbau has played an important role in the Lausitz region since 1846. It is also one of the most advanced breweries in the whole of Germany and is well known for its wide range of special beers.

BREWING SECRET The special beers have an international following.

Kirsch Porter
PORTER 4.2% ABV
A black beer with a cherry flavor and typical porter qualities. Malty and full-bodied.

Lausitzer Porter
PORTER 4.4% ABV
Typical porter with a dry, roasted malt taste. It is full-bodied and not too heavy; dark colored and a little bit sweet.

Bernard

5 Května č.1, 396 01 Humpolec,
CZECH REPUBLIC
www.bernard.cz

While reviving 16th-century
Humpolec brewery in 1991,
Stanislav Bernard and two
partners took the daring
decision to produce traditional
unpasteurized beers using
microfiltration. Since then,
awards and an expanding
export market have followed.

BREWING SECRET Bernard has its own
floor maltings and uses spring water.

Celebration / Sváteční Ležák
PREMIUM LAGER 5% ABV
Delicate herblike hop and yeast
aromas overlay a peppery bitterness
for a grassy finish.

Amber / Jantarový Ležák
AMBER BEER 4.4% ABV
Brewed using caramalt for a nutty
bitterness, offset by toffee aromas
and a honeyed palate.

Big Sky

5417 Trumpeter Way
Missoula, MT 59808, **USA**
www.bigskybrew.com

Three partners successfully combined a quality ale with a clever name (albeit one it had to defend in lawsuits lodged by Canadian brewer Moosehead) and an attractive label. Big Sky has grown quickly into a regional brewery selling beer from Alaska to Minnesota, three-quarters of it their flagship brown ale.

Moose Drool

BROWN ALE **5.3**% ABV
Dark fruits and nuts mingle with chocolate; sweetness moderated by earthy hop notes. Chocolate-brown with a medium body.

Scape Goat Pale Ale

PALE ALE **4.7**% ABV
Biscuity, fruity, and spicy on the palate, balanced by moderate bitterness. Short but dry finish.

Birrificio Italiano

Via Castello 51, 22070 Lurago
Marinon (CO), **ITALY**
www.birrificio.it

Agostino Arioli founded his
renowned brewpub in 1994 with
his brother Stefano and other
friends. His pils and bock soon
became cult favorites. He brews
a large range of seasonal beers
such as a sparkling blackcurrant
lager and a cask-conditioned
ale spiced with cinnamon and
ginger. The restaurant serves
great regional food and has
live music.

Scires
CHERRY ALE 7% ABV
Whole black Vignola cherries, lactic
bacteria, wild yeast, and wood chips
create this fantastic sour beer.

Fleurette
FLAVORED LIGHT ALE 3.7% ABV
Made with barley, wheat, and rye,
and flavored with rose and violet petals,
elderberry juice, black pepper, and
citrus honey.

Bitburger

Römermauer. 3, 54634 Bitburg/ Eifel, **GERMANY**
www.bitburger.de

Founded in 1817, Bitburger is a pilsner specialist. It is well known through international sponsorship of sporting events, and is widely regarded as the best brewery for pilsner on draft.

BREWING SECRET The company always uses two-row summer barley, and its testing brewery is unique in Germany.

Premium Pils
PILSNER 4.8% ABV
A clear, typical pilsner with a light, bitter taste; smooth, but very dry. On draft it is fresh and elegant.

Bitburger Light
PILSNER 2.8% ABV
The light sister of the premium. Though only 2.8% ABV, it is full-bodied, with a fresh cask taste.

Black Sheep

Masham, North Yorkshire,
HG4 4EN **ENGLAND**
www.blacksheepbrewery.com

The Theakston family has brewed
in Masham, North Yorkshire,
for six generations, but a loss
of independence led to Paul
Theakston stepping aside. He
then established Black Sheep
in a former maltings sitting high
above the Ure River. Since 1992,
Black Sheep has enjoyed
continuous growth, physically
and in reputation, resulting in a
£5m doubling of capacity in 2006.

Black Sheep Ale
BITTER 4.4% ABV
Full-flavored, with a rich, fruity aroma,
bitter-sweet malty taste, and long,
dry finish.

Riggwelter
PREMIUM BITTER 5.9% ABV
A strong, complex, fruity bitter,
with dashes of pear drops and hints
of liquorice.

J Boag & Son

39 William Street, Launceston,
Tasmania 7250, **AUSTRALI**a
www.boags.com.au

From a once-moribund regional
brewery, Boag's has ridden a
wave of popularity since the
launch of James Boag's Premium
Lager in 1994. Lagers comprise
the bulk of production, but
Boag's has rolled out some
fine limited-edition ales in
recent years. The brewery was
acquired by the Lion Nathan
group in late 2007.

Wizard Smith's Ale

BITTER ALE 5% ABV

A solid malt backbone, with toffee and
spicy hop notes, is rounded out by a
significant bitterness.

Bockor

Kwabrugstraat 5, B8510 Bellegem,
BELGIUM
www.bockor.be

This brewery is probably best
known for its Jacobins (would-be
lambics that use spontaneous
fermentation). However, the
brewery turns out a whole range
of other beers, not least a
traditional style oud bruin,
created by former head brewer
Omer Vander Ghinste. Bockor
is currently revamping the range
of beers.

Bellegems Bruin

MIXED FERMENTATION BEER 5.5% ABV
Oud bruin relies both on wild and
cultivated yeasts. The result: a beer in
which flavors of berries, wood, and lactic
sourness abound.

Bøgedal Bryghus

Høllundvej 9, DK-7100 Vejle,
DENMARK
www.boegedal.com

This farmhouse is the world's only commercial brewery producing the old Danish style of "Goodbeer," a strong, rich beer dating back to before the industrial age. The same recipe is always followed, and yet no two beers are alike, hence they are numbered rather than named.

BREWING SECRET Bøgedal is Scandinavia's only all-gravity brewery.

Brew No. 127
DARK ALE **6.3**% ABV
Smells of prunes and citrus. Fills the palate and lingers on with a faint smoky aftertaste.

Brew No. 121
PALE ALE **5.9**% ABV
Light amber in color with compact carbonation. Aromatic sweetness reaveals notes of honey, citrus, and fine wine.

Boon

Fonteinstraat 65,
B1520 Lembeek, **BELGIUM**
www.boon.be

In 1975, when lambic-based beers
and lambic brewers were dying
out, Frank Boon took over the De
Vits range. Deemed crazy, he still
proves his detractors wrong, by
constantly growing and
improving his business.

BREWING SECRET Most Boon beers
are deemed "oude," meaning "in the old
style" of unadulterated lambics.

Geuze Boon Mariage Parfait
GUEUZE 8% ABV
"Perfect marriage," meaning the lambics,
of course, resulting in the brewers'
favorite dry gueuze.

Boon Oude Kriek
KRIEKEN 6.5% ABV
A fully unsweetened krieken (sour
cherry) lambic, which makes this beer
a delight for tongue and eyes.

Boon Rawd

999 Samsen Road, Bangkok,
10300 **THAILAND**
www.boonrawd.co.th

Boon Rawd was founded in
1933 by Phraya Bhirom Bhakdi,
who had toured Germany and
Denmark to learn about brewing.
The brewery is still owned by the
Bhirom-Bhakdi family. The
company operates three
breweries in Thailand.

Singha
LAGER 6% ABV

A full-bodied barley malt beer with
a strong hop character. Clean to taste,
it complements spicy food.

Singha Light
LAGER 3.5% ABV

Lacks the complexity and vitality of its
stronger stablemate. It is pale yellow of
hue and thin to taste.

Boscos

Various locations in Tennessee
and Arkansas, **USA**
www.boscosbeer.com

Since 1992 this brewpub
chain has been a leader in
promoting greater knowledge
of beer in the mid-south. Its
pubs feature English-inspired
cask-conditioned ales, with
customers invited to participate
as cellermen.

BREWING SECRET Flaming Stone's
brewing process involves red-hot chunks
of granite being plunged into the wort to
caramelize the sugars.

Flaming Stone Beer
STEINBEER 4.8% ABV
Brewed in the manner of German stein
beers. Caramel, toffee, and nuts
throughout. Smoky, dry finish.

Hefeweizen
HEFEWEIZEN 4.8% ABV
Classic bubblegum and banana nose;
softer fruity (more banana) and creamy
flavors, with underlying spices including
light clove notes.

Bourganel

7 avenue Claude Expilly,
07600 Vals les Bains, **FRANCE**
www.bieres-bourganel.com

In 1997 Christian Bourganel,
a drinks distributor in the
Ardèche, decided to develop a
range of blonde artisan beers
flavored with regional produce.

BREWING SECRET Unusual ingredients
include chestnuts (*marrons*), bilberries
(*myrtilles*), nougat from Montélimar and
Verveine du Velay liqueur, which
is flavored with verbena.

Bourganel au Nougat
FLAVORED LAGER 5% ABV
An amazing nougat bouquet and, in the
mouth, the flavor of grilled almonds.

Bourganel aux Marrons
FLAVORED LAGER 5% ABV
An amber beer; elegant, very fruity and
refreshing, with a hint of vanilla as well
as chestnut.

Brains

Crawshay Street, Cardiff,
Glamorgan, CF10 1SP **WALES**
www.sabrain.com

A major force in regional brewing, Brains is tremendously proud of its Welsh heritage. Ales are produced in a traditional fashion at the company's landmark Cardiff Brewery, to which it was relocated in 2000 from the nearby Old Brewery, where the famous "pint of Brains" had been produced for more than 100 years.

Brains SA Gold
BEST BITTER 4.2% ABV
Its spirit aroma blends gentle malt and spiced hop with malt-rich and fruit flavors.

Brains Bitter
BITTER 3.7% ABV
Rich amber color, with subtle malt and crisp hop aromas. Well balanced, with some bitterness.

Brakspear

Witney, Oxfordshire,
OX28 4DP **ENGLAND**
www.brakspear.co.uk

The long-established Brakspear Brewery closed its Henley operation in 2002, but the production of its beers was taken on by Wychwood Brewery.

BREWING SECRET Wychwood uses Brakspear's original equipment to brew these beers, including the unique "double drop" wooden fermenting vessels, and its complex yeast strain.

Brakspear Bitter
BITTER 3.4% ABV

An initial malt and well-hopped bitterness develops into a bittersweet and fruity finish.

Brakspear Special
STRONG BITTER 4.3% ABV

Full-bodied, with a hint of sweetness and dry hop bitterness before finishing citrus-fruity.

Brahma

Rua São Cristóvão, 1221, São Cristóvão, Rio de Janeiro, **BRAZIL**
www.brahma.com

The Portuguese brought beer to Brazil at the beginning of the 19th century but it was Swiss immigrant Joseph Villager who first brewed Brahma in 1888. Named after the Hindu god, Brahma has grown to be one of the world's most drunk beers. The company is now part of Anheuser-Busch InBev.

Brahma
LAGER 4.8% ABV
Low in bitterness and light to drink, it has a subtle fruity aroma and no aftertaste.

Antarctica
LAGER 4.9% ABV
Light in color, bitterness, and aroma, it is an easy drinking beer.

BridgePort

1313 Northwest Marshall Street
Portland, OR 97209, **USA**
www.bridgeportbrew.com

BridgePort Brewing holds the trademark of Oregon's Oldest Craft Brewery, and its India Pale Ale has come to define the Northwest's beer character. Despite several expansions, it remains Portland-oriented. It dedicates each release of Old Knucklehead, its seasonal barley wine, to a different local personality.

India Pale Ale

INDIA PALE ALE 5.5% ABV
Citrussy from the outset. Solid malt backbone, delicate fruits (peaches and apples). Complex hoppy finish.

Black Strap Stout

STOUT 6% ABV
A rich blend of black strap molasses, chocolate and coffee, finishing with roasted bitterness.

Brinkhoff

Lütgendortmunder Hellweg 242,
44388 Dortmund, **GERMANY**
www.brinkhoffs.de

From its humble origins in
1844 as a small home brewery,
Brinkhoff has had more than
160 years of success, to become
a brand known far beyond its
hometown of Dortmund, one of
the beer capitals of the world.
Brinkhoff's No. 1 is a notable
name for every lover of the
special pilsners from this region.

Brinkhoff's No. 1

PILSNER 5% ABV

Typical bitter aromas of a pilsner.
Smooth, slightly sparkling, with
a golden-yellow color.

Brinkhoff's Radler

BEER BLEND 2.5% ABV

Honey-colored, sparkling, and pleasant
with citrus aromas; very refreshing and
not too sweet.

OREGON, USA

The term "Beervana" is often used to describe Oregon's culture of craft beer. Beer touring opportunities abound, and it would be possible to spend weeks traveling and never drink the same beer twice. This three-day trail starts in the seaside town of Newport, which is home to the iconic Rogue Ales brewery. It continues the next day with scenic stops on the way to Portland, then concludes with a full day in the Rose City. For more information visit www.oregonbeer.org.

DAY 1: NEWPORT AND ROGUE ALES

Rogue Ales Public House is located on OSU Drive, right in the center of the working seaport of Newport. There are plenty of bed and breakfasts to choose from in this friendly town, including Rogue's "Bed and Beer" apartments, above the public house. The public house is also the place to book in for one of the brewery tours, which commence at 3pm daily. *2320 OSU Drive, Newport (www.rogueales.com)*

DAY 2: PELICAN PUB & BREWERY

The scenic 48-mile (77-km) drive from Newport to Pacific City easily occupies a morning, so you should arrive just in time for lunch at the Pelican Pub & Brewery. The brewery-restaurant is located on the shoreline of Pacific City, where there are outstanding views of the oft-photographed Haystack Rock and Cape Kiwanda. *33180 Cape Kiwanda Drive, Pacific City (www.pelicanbrewery.com)*

DAY 2: GOLDEN VALLEY BREWERY & PUB

The scenic route to McMinnville passes through the Willamette Valley, one of the nation's premier wine-growing regions. The Golden Valley Brewery & Pub offers ales, sometimes aged in wine barrels. *980 East 4th St., McMinnville*

DAY 3: PORTLAND

With more than three dozen breweries in the metropolitan region, it is little wonder residents of Portland like to say they live in "Beervana." Here are some you could visit on Day 3 of this trail.

Hair of the Dog
This tiny brewery uses equipment not originally designed for brewing. Visits by appointment. *4509 SE 23rd Avenue, Portland (www.hairofthedog.com)*

Widmer
Visit the brewery's Gasthaus restaurant to sample the full line-up of beers—including the Alt intended to be the brewery flagship before its Hefeweizen became an American standard. The brewery offers tours on Fridays and Saturdays. *929 North Russell, Portland*

BridgePort (see p62)
Oregon's oldest surviving brewery helped turn the Pearl District into a hip locale. *1313 Northwest Marshall Street, Portland*

TRAIL OR TOUR STATS
3 days
230 km (142 miles)

0   20 miles
0km   30km

Higgins Brewpub

Greg Higgins uses local produce for his widely praised menu, which pairs well with Oregon beers and wines. *1239 SW Broadway, Portland*

Green Dragon Bistro and Pub

This relative newcomer quickly became an instant hit with a trendy crowd. Offers a constantly-changing selection of beers not necessarily found elsewhere, served by a knowledgeable staff. *928 SE 9th Avenue, Portland*

Horse Brass Pub

A Portland institution since 1976, the Horse Brass is a sprawling tribute to both the English pub and Oregon beer, offering 52 selections on draft. The pub is especially popular with the late-night crowd. *4534 SE Belmont Street, Portland*

Bristol

1647 South Tejon
Colorado Springs, CO 80906, **USA**
www.bristolbrewing.com

Since opening in 1994, Bristol Brewing has been the beer hub in Colorado Springs, as others have come and gone. It ventured into experimenting with barrels ahead of many US breweries.

BREWING SECRET It has won awards with a beer made using wild yeast and lactic acid bacteria from raspberries picked in nearby Cheyenne Canyon.

Winter Warlock
OATMEAL STOUT **6.5% ABV**
Toasted marshmallows and chocolate up front, creamy chocolate and roasted flavors on the palate.

Laughing Lab
SCOTTISH ALE **5.3% ABV**
Medium-bodied, with sweet notes of caramel and toffee and a lingering impression of smoke. Best on tap.

Brøckhouse

Høgevej 6, DK-3400 Hillerød,
DENMARK
www.broeckhouse.dk

A fast-growing and popular microbrewery to the north of Copenhagen, established in 2002. It was the goal of owner Allan Poulsen, a former IT engineer, to create something different from ordinary Danish pilsner.

BREWING SECRET Poulsen uses quality ingredients and British, German, and Belgian brewing traditions to create exciting and memorable brews.

Brøckhouse IPA
INDIAN PALE ALE **6%** ABV
Top-fermented ale brewed with three varieties of hops to achieve a sweet, balanced complexity.

Brøckhouse Esrum Kloster
ABBEY ALE **7.5%** ABV
Developed with the monks of Esrum Abbey. Strong nose; sweet, spicy flavor with hints of aniseed, lavender, rosemary, and juniper.

Brooklyn

1 Brewers Row
79 North 11th Street
Brooklyn, NY 11211, **USA**
www.brooklynbrewery.com

While Brooklyn Brewery pays homage to New York's rich brewing history, it is very much a 21st-century business, and occupies New York's first commercial building to derive all of its electricity from wind power. The brewery's bottled beers are made under contract in upstate New York, while brewmaster Garrett Oliver regularly produces seasonals and a reserve series at the brewery, sold on tap throughout the region.

Brooklyner Weisse
HEFEWEIZEN 5.1% ABV
Effervescent and banana-fruity from the start, backed up with spices, hops, and gentle clove notes.

Local 1
BELGIAN STRONG GOLDEN ALE 9% ABV
An explosion of aromas and flavors of fruits and spices, and a complex texture, all brought together with a chalky-dry finish.

Brouwerij 't IJ

Funenkade 7, 1018 AL Amsterdam,
NETHERLANDS
www.brouwerijhetij.nl

Amsterdam's favorite micro is
now the city's oldest brewery,
even though it was founded only
in 1985. Strong Belgian-style ales
form the backbone of the output,
though there's also a pils and a
witbier. Set in an old windmill,
the taproom is thronged on warm
summer afternoons, its outdoor
seating taken up by drinkers
enjoying the lowest beer prices
in Amsterdam.

Turbock
DOPPELBOCK 9% ABV
Packed with dark fruits and molasses
sweetness, the trademark IJ spiciness
adds a dimension not found in
German bocks.

Columbus
STRONG ALE 9% ABV
A balance of biscuity malt, coriander,
lemon, and resinous, minty hops.
Assertive, but not overpowering.

BrowArmia

Ul. Królewska 1,
Warszawa, 00-065, **POLAND**
www.browarmia.pl

Opened in 2005, this fine
brewpub has a vibrant
atmosphere—busy, convivial, and
loud on music nights. Polish food
with a modern twist is a specialty
to match the beers on tap. Six
beers are currently brewed in the
smart cellar brewery, with six
more planned for the future.

Pszenciczne
PALE ALE 4.8% ABV
Not quite a Burton ale, it is strongly
hopped in the kettle before being
dry-hopped in the lagering tank.

Raspberry Wheat Beer
WHEAT BEER 5% ABV
The house wheat beer is in the
Bavarian style, with the addition
of fresh raspberries. The fruit adds
a refreshing, zesty tartness.

Bucher Bräu

Elsenthaler Str. 5-7,
9441 Grafenau, **GERMANY**
www.bucher-braeu.de

A medium-sized brewery
that moved to the heart of the
Bavarian Forest in 1982 after
outgrowing its premises in the
center of Grafenau. It has been
owned by the Bucher family since
1863 (now in its fifth generation).

BREWING SECRET The natural
cloudiness of the Hefeweizen comes from
the yeast added at the time of bottling.

Grafenauer Hefeweizen
WHEAT BEER 5.2% ABV
Fresh and sparkling. The light taste
of yeast is fine and aromatic. There
is a little sweetness.

Helles
LAGER 4.9% ABV
Clear yellow beer, slightly bitter,
with a reasonable sweetness, and
a taste of the finest hops. A rather
strong but rounded finish.

Budels

Nieuwstraat 9,
6020 AA Budel, **NETHERLANDS**
www.budels.nl

Budels is among the few established, predominantly bottom-fermenting Dutch breweries. Started in 1870, the business is currently run by the fourth generation of the founding Aerts family.

BREWING SECRET In recent years Budels has diversified into top-fermenting beers, such as kölsch, altbier, and an abbey-style dubbel.

Budels Lager
PILS 5% ABV
A gentle, piney hop aroma is followed by fruity, sweetish taste; perhaps closer to a helles than a pils.

Budels Capucijn
ABBEY-STYLE DOUBLE 6.5% ABV
Sweet toasted malt aromas are complemented by bitterness, dates, and the merest hint of smoke.

Budweiser Budvar

Karolíny Světle 4, 370 21
České Budějovice,
CZECH REPUBLIC
www.original-budweiser.cz

The town of České Budějovice (Budweis) has been a home of brewing since 1265. Today, the Budějovický (Budweiser) Budvar product name has Protected Geographical Indicator status within the EU (like Cognac and Parma ham), but in the US, where Anheuser-Busch's Budweiser is trademarked, it is called Czechvar.

Budweiser Budvar / Czechvar
PREMIUM LAGER 5% ABV
Spritzy, with an attractive head, floral and grapefruit fruitiness on the nose, and a dry, biscuit malt palate.

Czech Dark Lager
DARK BEER 4.7% ABV
Its distinct malty flavor develops a cinnamon spiciness before rolling into biscuit undertones.

Carib

Eastern Main Road,
Champs Fleurs, **TRINIDAD**
www.caribbeer.com

The sole brewery on Trinidad
since 1957, Carib has formed
business links with InBev,
Carlsberg, and Diageo—the
owner of Guinness. The company
also has breweries in Grenada,
St. Kitts, and Nevis. The British
brought commercial brewing to
Trinidad just after World War I;
the local taste favors sweet lagers
and strong stouts.

Carib Lager
LAGER 5.2% ABV
Pale, but full-bodied with a rich head
formation. Slightly aromatic, balanced
between sweet and bitter.

Carib Stag
LAGER 5.9% ABV
European style lager. It is has a pale
golden straw color with a rich head
formation. Very sweet.

Cascade

131 Cascade Road, South Hobart,
Tasmania 7004, **AUSTRALIA**
www.cascadebrewery.com.au

Australia's oldest operating
brewery, complete with on-site
maltings, is also the most
striking, with the castellated
sandstone building nestled in
the foothills of the sometimes
snow-capped Mount Wellington.
Now part of the Foster's empire,
Cascade attracts tens of
thousands of beer lovers
annually to its visitor center.

Cascade Stout
MEDIUM STOUT **5.8**% ABV
Coffee notes up front, with milk chocolate
on the palate, followed by a moderately
bitter finish.

Cascade Blonde
SUMMER ALE **4.8**% ABV
Clean and crisp, with a hint of citrus
hop flavor.

Castelain

13 rue Pasteur,
62410 Bénifontaine, **FRANCE**
www.chti.com

Founded in 1926, this family brewery was passed into the hands of Yves and Annick Castelain from their parents in 1978. Under the name of Ch'ti (local patois for a northerner), they have developed a range of strong, mellow lager beers with a long, cold secondary fermentation period.

Maltesse
PREMIUM LAGER 7.7% ABV
Blonde, rich, and strong, with a taste of barley, and an appealing hint of bitterness in the finish.

Ch'ti Blonde
LAGER 6.4% ABV
Full-bodied, with just enough bitterness to be very refreshing. Mellow and tasty.

Castle / SAB

65 Park Lane, Sandown,
Sandtona, **SOUTH AFRICA**
www.sablimited.co.za

SAB—South African Breweries—
was founded in 1895 and began
producing its Castle Lager brand
in the mining town of
Johannesburg. The company
soon became the biggest brewer
in southern Africa. In 2002,
SAB bought Miller Brewing in
the US, and as SABMiller it has
become one of the biggest global
drinks companies.

Castle Lager

LAGER 5% ABV

Award-winning lager made from African
Gold Barley and Southern Star hops. It is
brewed in nine countries and sold in 40.

Castle Milk Stout

MILK STOUT 6% ABV

Dark, highly-hopped, strong stout with
a complex taste of roasted black malts,
coffee, and caramel.

Cereuro— Cervejeira Europeia

Estrada da Portela nº8,
2795 – 643 Carnaxide, **PORTUGAL**
www.sumolis.pt

Part of soft drinks manufacturer
Grupo Sumol, this brewery
was set up after the revolution
of 1974, when the brewing
industry was nationalized.
It went into private ownership
in the 1990s. The company also
brews Magna, an interesting
German-style dark beer, and
markets Grolsch in Portugal.

Tagus
LAGER 5.4% ABV
A clear golden color, this beer is rich and
malty with caramel overtones. Its estery
nose hints of its alcoholic strength and its
warming finish.

Cervesur

Av. De la Cultura 725, Cusco, **PERU**

Based in southern Peru in the Andes, the company, which is of German origin, has been brewing since 1898 and is now part of SABMiller. It is currently being merged with SABMiller's other Peruvian company Backus & Johnson. Its main brand, Cusqueña, is Peru's best-selling lager.

BREWING SECRET The water for brewing comes from a source high in the Andes.

Cusqueña
LAGER 5% ABV
Pronounced "Cus-Ken-Ya," the beer is crisp and refreshing, with a lingering lemon aroma.

Cēsu Alus

Aldaru laukums 1,
Cēsis, 4101 **LATVIA**
www.cesualus.lv

Cēsu Alus was founded in 1879
and is the oldest brewery in
Latvia. In 1999 it was purchased
by the Estonian brewer A. Le
Coq. It is now one of the largest
brewers in Latvia. It has a new,
state-of-the-art brewhouse and
further huge investment is being
planned. The town is renowned
for its beer festival, knights'
tournaments, and open-air
theater performances.

Cēsu Premium
LAGER 5.2% ABV
Sweet chocolate taste with hints of
aromatic vanilla. In Latvia, balsam is
commonly used to flavor drinks.

Cēsu Balsam Porter
PORTER 6% ABV
A pale golden color, it has hints of
sweet grass and hops on the nose.

Chimay

8, Route Charlemagne,
B6464 Baileux, **BELGIUM**
www.chimay.com

Though the bottling is done in
Baileux, the brewery is still in the
monastery at Forges-les-Chimay.
Since 1861, monks have brewed
here, but Chimay became the
leading Trappist brewery
through Père Theodore, who
went to Leuven University to
study brewing in a contemporary
way. Chimay never stopped
growing and is vital to the
economy of the region.

Chimay Tripel
ABBEY ALE 8% ABV
Sweet, grapey taste, with bittering hops
and herbal qualities; not entirely unlike
a dry white wine.

Grande Réserve / Bleue
BELGIAN STRONG ALE 9% ABV
Roasted malts, with some quite dominant
bitterness, and dark, ripe fruit (plums,
blue grapes), and pears.

La Choulette

18 rue des Écoles,
59111 Hordain, **FRANCE**
www.lachoulette.com

Founded in 1885, this farmhouse brewery is a rare survivor from the thousands of breweries that existed in the region in the late 19th century. Alain Dhaussy, the current brewer, has succeeded in creating artisan beers of real quality, faithful to the traditions of northern France, but with a real sense of innovation too.

Choulette Framboise
FRUIT BEER 6% ABV
Refreshing, with a slight sourness. The note of ripe raspberries is present, but not too intrusive.

Porte Du Hainaut Ambrée
AMBER ALE 7% ABV
Medium-bodied fruity beer, with flavors of cooked apples, pears, and caramel; slight bitterness.

Coopers

461 South Road, Regency Park,
Adelaide, South Australia 5010,
AUSTRALIA
www.coopersbrewery.com.au

While most Australian breweries
were progressively "lagerized"
during the 20th century, this
family-run Adelaide brewing
dynasty kept knocking out
cloudy, bottle-conditioned
ales and stouts. Since opening
a new expanded brewery in
2001, surging demand for their
beers has driven them to
become the country's third-
largest beermaker.

Coopers Sparkling Ale

AUSTRALIAN PALE ALE 5.8% ABV
Cloudy; fruity aromatics with a hint of
peaches; rounded, dry, yeasty finish.

Coopers Extra Stout

DRY STOUT 6.4% ABV
Espresso and bitter chocolate notes, with
banana hints too; robustly bitter finish.

Coors

311 10th Street
Golden, CO 80401, **USA**
www.coors.com

Although it merged with Molson, and that company now partners SABMiller in the US, Coors has continued to develop less mainstream beers. Its Blue Moon line competes with the largest craft brands, and its SandLot Brewery, within the Coors Field baseball stadium in Denver, regularly offers outstanding traditional lagers.

Blue Moon Belgian White

WITBIER 5.4% ABV

Citrussy sweet nose, spicy with notes of celery. Some wheat sourness, finishing on the sweet side.

Barmen Pilsner

PILSNER 5% ABV

Beautiful billowing head when poured correctly. Rich with Saaz hops, floral and spicy. Pleasantly grainy, with a long, bitter finish.

Cornelyshaff

Maison 37,9753 Heinerscheid,
LUXEMBOURG
www.cornelyshaff.lu

Situated in a nature park,
Cornelyshaff comprises a
popular bar, restaurant, and
hotel, as well as a brewery that
is open to visitors. It is modern,
gleaming, and energy efficient—
the cooperative that owns it
prides itself on minimizing its
environmental impact. The bar
and restaurant showcase the
beers and much farm produce
from the area.

Ourdaller Waïssen Tarwebier
WITBIER **4.6%** ABV
An unfiltered, cloudy wheat beer;
assertive in character, it is full of spice.

Kornelysbéier
RYE BEER **4.2%** ABV
A spicy aroma gives way to a strongly
flavored deep, earthy taste brought on
by the use of rye grain.

Crailsheimer Engelbräu

Haller Str. 29, 74564 Crailsheim, **GERMANY**
www.engelbier.de

When this brewery was founded by Georg Fach in 1738, Crailsheim had 4,000 inhabitants and 13 breweries. Fach was not to know that his company would become one of the most successful in the country.

BREWING SECRET A survey of what women like in a beer led to the creation of the First Lady brand.

First Lady
DUNKLER BOCK **5.9**% ABV
Mild, lightly bitter, and with a harmonious malty aroma.

Kellerbier Dunkel
DUNKEL **5.3**% ABV
Beautiful mahogany color; aromas of malt and yeast; full-bodied, with a taste that is both sweet and pleasantly bitter.

Creemore Springs

139 Mill Street, Creemore,
Ontario, L0M 1G0, **CANADA**
www.creemoresprings.com

Ownership by Molsons since
2005 has done little to lessen the
independence of this 100-year-old
brewery. The town of Creemore
nestles between the curiously
named Mad and Noisy rivers.
Every August the brewery
is a sponsor of a town-center
party called the Copper Kettle
Festival. Regular brewery tours
are run.

Premium Lager
LAGER 5% ABV
Soft malt and fruit flavors give way to
nutty overtones and a dry hoppy finish.

Urbock
BOCK 6% ABV
Dark brown, with a sweet, nutty texture;
fruit aromas can be found as the beer
warms in the glass.

Deschutes

901 Southwest Simpson Avenue,
Bend, OR 97702, **USA**
www.deschutesbrewery.com

What began with a brewpub in
1988 quickly expanded with a
separate production facility
that's grown into one of the
nation's largest craft breweries.
As well as selling a full line of
beers with notable hop character
throughout the western US,
Deschutes still operates its
original brewpub in downtown
Bend and another in Portland.
A Bond Street Series of special
beer releases, developed "at the
pub," has further widened the
brewery's portfolio.

Mirror Pond
PALE ALE **5.2%** ABV
Grapefruit and fresh flowers at the outset.
Light, clean biscuit on the palate, with
generous hop flavor.

Inversion IPA
INDIA PALE ALE **6.8%** ABV
A swirl of hop aromas (particularly
orange zest). Solid, biscuity malt holds
its own against bracing bitterness.

Desnoes and Geddes

214 Spanish Town, Kingston,
JAMAICA
www.jamaicadrinks.com

Now owned by global drinks giant
Diageo, Desnoes and Geddes was
established by two friends,
Eugene Desnoes and Thomas
Geddes, who set up a soft drink
plant in 1918 and began brewing
in 1927 with Red Stripe.

BREWING SECRET Red Stripe was
originally produced as an English ale.
It didn't become popular until it was
offered as a chilled lager instead.

Dragon Stout
SWEET STOUT 7.5% ABV
Having been primed with sugar on
bottling, the flavor is malty, with
a distinct note of molasses.

Dragon Gold
LAGER 5.5% ABV
Yellow in color, it has a grainy aroma,
a crisp, clean taste, and is best drunk
very cold.

Dětenice

Pivovar Dětenice, 507 24 Dětenice,
CZECH REPUBLIC
www.krcmadetenice.cz

The castle-based brewery—once owned by the Prague chapter of the Knights of Malta—closed in 1955 after several years of nationalization, and reopened only in 2000.

BREWING SECRET Beers are brewed in direct-fired vessels and are filtered through straw, fermented in wooden vats, then lagered in oak barrels.

Svetlé Detenické Pivo 12°
PREMIUM LAGER 4% ABV
Aromatically floral, finely structured body; sweet malt and honey influences, and hoppy afterglow.

Tmavé Detenicke Pivo 13°
DARK BEER 4% ABV
A typically full-bodied dark lager; malty, some spice, and faintly bitter toward the finish.

Dogfish Head

6 Cannery Village Center
Milton, DE 19968, **USA**
www.dogfish.com

Dogfish Head has found
a national audience for its
"extreme beers." These have
included ales developed using
research from archaeologists
and recipes featuring unusual
ingredients, from chicory to
chilies. The brewery recently
installed the largest wooden
brewing vessels built in the US
since before Prohibition. Dogfish
still operates a brewpub in
Rehoboth Beach, where founder
Sam Calagione started in 1995.

Midas Touch
HISTORIC BEER 9% ABV
The ingredients—white Muscat grapes,
honey, and saffron—create layers of
flavor, melded with subtle acidity.

60 Minute IPA
INDIA PALE ALE 6% ABV
Flagship session beer brewed with
Warrior, Amarillo, and "Mystery Hop
X," and brimming with citrus flavors.

Dreher

Magladi ut 17, Budapest, **HUNGARY**
www.dreher.hu

For many years this brewery was run by Anton Dreher, one of the great beer innovators. In the mid-19th century, he developed the technology to ferment beer at low temperatures and created a new kind of malty amber beer, called Vienna lager. For his achievements, Dreher was dubbed "The King of Beer." The company is now owned by SABMiller.

Dreher Classic

PILSNER 5.5% ABV

With a crisp, fresh aroma, this is a bitter, golden-yellow beer with an aroma of hops and a hint of malt.

Dreher Bak

DUNKLER BOCK 7.3% ABV

A rich, full-bodied dark beer, notes of caramel and malt, reminiscent of bittersweet chocolate.

Dubuisson

28, Chaussée de Mons,
B7904 Pipaix-Leuze, **BELGIUM**
www.br-dubuisson.com

Leuze is a town with three breweries, two of them in the Pipaix village. Dubuisson is probably the most dynamic, and its location, next to a major road, has made their brewery tap a very successful venture. The brewery excels in high alcohol ales, so extreme caution is advised when drinking these beers.

Bush Prestige

BELGIAN STRONG ALE 13% ABV
This oak-aged version of the Ambrée is a true marvel in balance, despite its impressive strength.

Bush Ambrée

BELGIAN STRONG ALE 12% ABV
In some markets known as "Scaldis," this is a treacherously drinkable alcohol-bomb.

Ducato

Via Strepponi 50/A, 43010 Roncole
Verdi di Busseto (PR), **ITALY**
www.birrificiodelducato.it

Young brewer Giovanni Campari
set up his microbrewery in 2007
near Giuseppe Verdi's birthplace,
not far from Parma. He proved
his skills from the outset,
brewing four beers full of
character. Further new lines
are confirming Ducato as one
of the most promising Italian
craft breweries.

New Morning
SAISON 5.6% ABV
Amazing saison, flavored with camomile
flowers. Easy-drinking and thirst-
quenching, with lovely earthy notes.

AFO
AMERICAN PALE ALE 5.2% ABV
AFO means "Ale For the Obsessed" and is
dedicated to hop lovers. Nice citrus fruit
aromas, caramel notes.

Duck-Rabbit

4519 W Pine Street
Farmville, NC 27828, **USA**
www.duckrabbitbrewery.com

Known for darkly intense beers, this is one of several small breweries that have thrived since North Carolina changed its law to allow beer stronger than 6% ABV. Duck-Rabbit's distinctive logo is based on an illustration by philosopher Ludwig Wittgenstein.

BREWING SECRET These quirky brewers say "We sing softly to the yeast."

Baltic Porter
BALTIC PORTER 9% ABV
Caramel, toffee, blackcurrants, and other dark fruits, perfectly blended. Smooth, with restrained bitterness.

Milk Stout
STOUT 5.7% ABV
A well-integrated combination of roasted coffee beans and chocolate, held together by a creamy palate. Sweet, but not too sweet.

Dugges Ale & Porterbryggeri

Möbelgatan 3, SE-43133 Mölndal, **SWEDEN**
www.dugges.se

The brewery was founded in 2005 by Mikael Dugge Engström. His series of beers include Gothenburg, marrying old Swedish traditions with British and American inspiration, and Express Yourself, a collection of specialty brews with names like Holy Cow (an IPA) and Fuggedaboudit! (a brown ale).

Dugges Avenyn Ale
AMERICAN PALE ALE 5% ABV
Aromas of hops, flowers, and citrus fruits; flavors of grapes, pine, and a hint of caramel.

High Five!
INDIAN PALE ALE 7.5% ABV
Dark amber. Intense hop aroma; notes of strawberry jam, pine, and chocolate, and a dry bitterness.

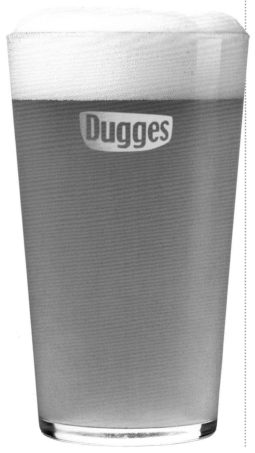

Dupont

Brasserie Dupont, 5 Rue Basse,
B7904 Tourpes-Leuze, **BELGIUM**
www.brasserie-dupont.com

Western-Hainaut enjoys rich soil,
and farmsteads here were huge—
usually operating a brewery in
the winter, making beer to be
consumed on the land in summer
(hence the style of beer known as
saison). Brasserie Dupont became
solely a brewery, but owner Olivier
Dedeycker has re-engaged with
the history of the land, by
reintroducing farming and
cheese-making into this
marvellous brewery.

Avec Les Bons Vœux

SEASONAL WINTER ALE 9.5% ABV

Once a complimentary winter ale, but so
superb that it is now brewed year round.
Barnyard and earthy aromas mingle with
citrus zest. Grainy flavor: fresh white
bread with nuts, spices, and walnut oil.

Saison Dupont

SAISON 6.5% ABV

Formerly brewed in winter with the hot
summer months in mind—hence a dry,
refreshingly light brew.

BRUSSELS, BELGIUM

"B" is for Belgium, Brussels, and Beer. Today, Belgian beers can be drunk worldwide, but the very best place to embrace Belgian beer culture is in Brussels itself, with its unique cafés, bars, and brasseries.

1 TOONE

The Beer Temple (*Rue Marché Aux Herbes 56*) is one of the world's best beer shops. It stocks most of Belgium's artisanal brewers. It is close to a narrow alleyway that forms the entrance to Toone, a puppet theater with a bar. The walls of this hidden gem are adorned with staring marionettes and the atmosphere is as good as the Kwak beer served here—in the correct glass of course.
6 Impasse Schuddevelde, off 21 Petit Ruedes Bouchers, Brussels

2 GRAND PLACE

Brussels' famous Grand Place is home to the Belgian Brewers Association and Brewery Museum—both occupy the opulent Brewers House. Several bars surround the square, but there are even better places to drink nearby. In September the square hosts an annual beer festival.

3 POECHENELLEKELDER

Opposite one of the world's most improbable tourist attractions, the Manneken Pis, is the Poechenellekelder. Loved by the people of Brussels, the bar has a list of 90 fine beers—a perfect introduction to the world of Belgian beers.
5 Rue du Chêne, Brussels

TRAIL OR TOUR STATS
2 hours, plus drinking time
7 miles (10 km)

0 — 200 yards
0 — 200m

4 IN 'T SPINNEKOPKE

Away from Grand Place, but not too far, can be found In 't Spinnekopke. "The Little Spiders Head" is a small, intimate two-bar restaurant and café. It is as Bruxellois as you can get and has to be one of the best places in Brussels to eat and drink beer. Chef Jean Rodriguez prides himself on pairing food and beer superbly. *1 Place du Jardin aux Fleurs, Brussels*

5 DELIRIUM

Ilot Sacré is a clamor of medieval lanes and fish restaurants with outrageous menu boards, and energetic and sometimes insistent waiters trying to coerce people inside to dine. Down one such alley is Delirium. Don't wait at your table for service, go to the bar, which claims to stock more than 2,000 beers. *4a Impasse de la Fidélité, Brussels*

6 MORTE SUBITE

Along the road is Galeries Royales St Hubert. Once the world's largest covered shopping mall, it leads the way to Morte Subite—a magnificent Art Nouveau bar, which is said to be the best surviving fin-de-siecle long bar in the world. Here is the place to try wildly fermented lambic or gueuze beers with a plate of *tête pressée* (brawn) or *kip kap* (pig cheeks). *7 Rue Montagne aux Herbes Potageres, Brussels*

7 BIER CIRCUS

Up the hill from Central Station is Bier Circus. This is the place to seek out beers from Belgium's growing band of artisanal brewers and experience the creative diversity of Belgian brewing. But take some friends with you—many of the beers are served only in 75cl bottles. *89 Rue de l'Enseignement, Brussels*

Duvel Moortgat

Breendonkdorp 58-66, B2870
Breendonk-Puurs, **BELGIUM**
www.duvel.be

Started as a small family brewery, Moortgat continued producing top-fermented ale at a time when everywhere lager reigned. The Moortgat ale evolved into the iconoclastic Duvel, a beer that has become so popular that the brewery group renamed itself. Moortgat now owns breweries in Belgium and abroad.

Duvel

BELGIAN STRONG ALE 8.5% ABV
Sometimes dubbed "red," to distinguish it from the filtered version, this ultra dry ale hides its potency as no other.

Maredsous 8°

BROWN ABBEY ALE 8% ABV
Arguably the best from the Maredsous Abbey range. Estery, fruity notes, and tobacco leaf.

Duyck

113 route Nationale, 59144 Jenlain,
FRANCE
www.duyck.com

Originally a farmhouse brewery,
Duyck was established in 1922,
producing beers in the northern
bière de garde style—brewed
and bottled in the winter for
laying down and drinking in
the summer. In the 1950s, the
family began bottling their
beers in recycled champagne
bottles. Raymond Duyck,
the present manager, is the
fourth generation of this family
of brewers.

Jenlain Ambrée

AMBER ALE 7.5% ABV

Full-bodied, with a hint of bitterness,
the mellowness of roasted malt and
aromas of stewed prunes and caramel.
A perfect accompaniment to food, but
also an ingredient in rustic local dishes
such as *Carbonnade Flamande* (beef
cooked in beer).

Echigo

3970 Fukui, Nishiura-ku, Niigata
City, Niigata 953-0076, **JAPAN**
www.echigo-beer.jp

The brewers of the venerable
Tsurukame saké of Niigata
opened Japan's first
microbrewery in February of 1995
to great fanfare. Operations have
expanded from the original
brewpub to a large-scale brewery
with canning line today. While the
canned products are well
regarded, the more expensive
small-production bottled products
are even more highly prized.

Echigo Pilsener

PILSNER 5% ABV

This reasonably priced craft beer has
a rich malty flavor, moderate bitterness,
and a clean, quick finish.

Echigo Stout

STOUT 7% ABV (PREVIOUSLY 5%)

Higher gravity and more care in
the brewing of this beer results
in a brilliant interplay of rich,
roasty flavors.

Eel River

1777 Alamar Way
Fortuna, CA 95540, **USA**
www.eelriverbrewing.com

Eel River had been around less than five years when, in 2000, it became the first certified organic brewery in the US. The brewpub added a production brewery in nearby Scotia in 2007, moving into an abandoned mill. The new brewery is 100 percent powered by biomass—that is, mill waste such as wood chippings, and spent grain from brewing.

Organic Porter

PORTER **6.3**% ABV
Malty and creamy with chocolate aromas and flavors, and lesser notes of roast coffee beans. Robust.

Triple Exultation

OLD ALE **9.7**% ABV
Not organic. A complex nose of rich caramel-toffee and fruit, then piney hops assert themselves.

Eggenberg

Eggenberg 1,
A-4655 Vorchdorf, **AUSTRIA**
www.schloss-eggenberg.at

Schloss Eggenberg is a small
castle in Upper Austria that
has been brewing for more
than 500 years. A broad range
of lagers (including a non-
alcoholic one) are produced
for the local market, and some
fine bock beers are brewed
for export; these include an
urbock and even a blonde
version of the traditionally
dark Samichlaus beer.

Samichlaus
DOPPELBOCK 14% ABV
Intense malt aroma, with noticeable
alcohol. Sweet and fruity (dried
cherries, figs, and plums); very little
hop character present.

Hopfenkönig
PILSNER 5.1% ABV
Very pale, with a firm head and haylike
spicy hop aromas. Light body followed by
some dry bitterness.

Eggenberg

Latrán 27, 38115, Český Krumlov,
CZECH REPUBLIC
www.eggenberg.cz

Nowhere but in Bohemia could two towns merge over brewing disputes. Years of arguing about wheat beer privileges were resolved simply by uniting neighbors Latrán and Krumlov, and establishing a single brewery. Over time, the brewery passed from the Eggenberg family to the Schwarzenbergs and down the centuries to its present owners, Dionex.

Eggenberg Světlý Ležák
PREMIUM LAGER 5% ABV
Powerfully floral with sweet butterscotch notes; zesty, firm, and delightfully balanced to a bitter finish.

Eggenberg Tmavý Ležák
DARK BEER 4.2% ABV
Deep and dark, with a hop pungency, then a malty caramel and toffee bittersweet palate.

Einbecker

Papenstr. 4, 37574 Einbeck,
GERMANY
www.einbecker.com

The story goes that, in 1521,
Martin Luther said that
Einbecker's beer was his favorite.
In 1612, Bavarian dukes engaged
a master brewer from Einbeck,
whose beer eventually became
known as bock, in a corruption
of the name Einbeck.

Ur-Bock Hell

BOCK **6.5%** ABV
The pale malt and fine hops give
this classic bock a hearty taste.

Einbecker Spezial

EXPORT **5.2%** ABV
Has the typical golden-yellow color
of an export beer. Has a fine, slightly
sweet flavor.

Emerson's Brewery

14 Wickliffe Street, Dunedin,
NEW ZEALAND
www.emersons.co.nz

New Zealand's most awarded micro offers an enviable portfolio of year-round beers, as well as seasonal specialties such as Taieri George, a spiced dark ale, and a US pale ale featuring American hops.

BREWING SECRET Emerson's delightful session beer called Bookbinder Bitter is available only on tap.

Emerson's Old 95
BARLEY WINE 7% ABV
Robust bottle conditioned ale, with rich, toffeelike malt and resiny hops. Will reward careful cellaring.

Emerson's Organic Pilsner
NEW WORLD PILSNER 4.9% ABV
Bursting with passion fruit and citrus. A showcase for New Zealand's Riwaka hop variety.

Felinfoel

Llanelli, Carmarthenshire,
SA14 8LB **WALES**
www.felinfoel-brewery.com

Sitting astride the Liedi River
and leaning heavily on the
industrial traditions of south
Wales—and its workers' thirsts—
Felinfoel Brewery has been in
existence since 1878. It is
famed for producing Britain's
first canned beer in 1935.
Extensive modernization
came in the 1970s, but
Felinfoel is still family-owned.

Double Dragon
BITTER **4.2%** ABV
Invitingly rich in color, malty and
subtly hopped, with an evenly
balanced, full-drinking nature.

Cambrian Bitter
BITTER **3.9%** ABV
Labeled "a good, honest Welsh bitter,"
the bitter is full-flavored, with balanced
malt and hop aromas.

Fiege

Moritz Fiege, Scharnhorststr. 21-25,
44787 Bochum, **GERMANY**
www.moritzfiege.de

"We are a classic regional
brewery" says Hugo Fiege, the
boss of the company. He sees his
brewery as an ambassador for the
Ruhr region. It is an institution
offering typical local beers—
inhabitants of the Ruhr love their
beer. There is little chance of a
big global player acquiring Fiege.

Moritz Fiege Pils
PILSNER 4.9% ABV
A classic pilsner with bitter aromas of
good hops, a light malty taste, and a fine
dry structure.

Schwarzbier
SCHWARZBIER 4.9% ABV
Elegant and with a malty sweetness,
this coffee-colored beer has light
bitter aromas of fine hops.

Finlandia

Suokulmantie 237, Matku,
Forsaa FI-31110, **FINLAND**
www.finlandiasahti.fi

Finlandia is a specialist brewer
of *sahti*, a traditional Finnish
home-brew made with rye and
other grains, flavored with
juniper twigs and berries. Beer
enthusiasts can sample Finlandia
Sahti in Helsinki at St. Urho's
Pub and the Restaurant Savotta.
The best time to do so is during
Helsinki's Sahti Week, which
takes place in May each year.

Sahti Strong
SAHTI 10% ABV
Sweet and somewhat oily on the
palate; the juniper nose gives way
to a bubblegum aftertaste.

Tavallinen
SAHTI 8% ABV
A deep chestnut color, with a heavy
juniper nose and a hint of blackcurrant.

Flensburger

Munketoft 12, 24937 Flensburg,
GERMANY
www.flensburger.de

Five citizens of Flensburg
founded this brewery in 1888.
During the 1970s, the brewery's
reputation was enhanced when
a comedian kept referring to a
"Flasch Flens" in his act. The
term came to be used for a bottle
of Flensburger, which at the time
was the only German beer to use
clip-top bottles.

Flensburger Pils
PILSNER 4.8% ABV
A typical golden pilsner—malty,
refreshing, and with slightly bitter
aromas of hops in the finish.

Kellerbier
KELLERBIER 4.8% ABV
Amber and cloudy, like all kellerbiers,
the Flensburger version is full-bodied
and tastes naturally fresh, slightly
sweet, and has a dry finish.

Flossmoor Station

1035 Sterling Avenue
Flossmoor, IL 60422, **USA**
www.flossmoorstation.com

Brewers Matt Van Wyk and
Andrew Mason have expanded on
what barrel-ageing pioneer Todd
Ashman started at Flossmoor
Station Brewing. They offer a
wide range of award-winning
beers in a pub housed in a former
train station. The brewery
recently launched a small
range of bottled beers.

Pullman Brown Ale
BROWN ALE 7% ABV
Brewed with hand-toasted malts and
molasses. A full-bodied blend of
chocolate, toffee, and dark fruit.

De Wilde Zuidentrein
SOUR ALE 7% ABV
A Flanders brown ale, aged in an oak
wine barrel on fresh raspberries for a
year, dosed with wild yeasts.

Flying Dog

2401 Blake Street
Denver, CO 80205, **USA**
www.flyingdogales.com

With labels by British illustrator
Ralph Steadman, and the "gonzo"
spirit of the late Hunter S.
Thompson (both friends of
founder George Stranahan),
Flying Dog is not your average
brewery. The original brewpub
was founded in Aspen but is now
headquartered in Denver, while
the company moved brewing
operations to Frederick in
Maryland in 2008.

Gonzo Imperial Porter
PORTER 9% ABV
Rummy, chocolatey, and almost sweet
before dry cocoa flavors and solid hop
bitterness kick in.

Doggie Style Pale Ale
PALE ALE 5.3% ABV
A fragrant mixture of fresh fruits to start.
Citrus accentuates fruit in the middle,
well balanced by biscuity malt. Clean,
dry finish.

Füchschen

Ratinger Str. 28, 40213 Düsseldorf,
GERMANY
www.fuechschen.de

Altbier has been a favored brew
at Füchschen since 1848. The
fourth generation of the family
is in charge. There have been
some changes since 1995,
including the installation
of new brewing equipment.

BREWING SECRET The Düsseldorf
carnival in February is a good
opportunity to sample the altbier.

Füchschen Alt
ALTBIER 4.5% ABV
Dark mahogany in color, this typical
Düsseldorfer is malty with a very
intense aroma of hops. Slightly
carbonated, and fresh.

Silberfüchsen
WHEAT BEER 5.4% ABV
A northern-style wheat beer, less sweet
than its Bavarian counterpart. Smooth,
fruity, and sparkling.

Fuller's

Chiswick Lane South, London,
W4 2QB **ENGLAND**
www.fullers.co.uk

London's last remaining
traditional family brewer,
Fuller's has been based at the
historic Griffin Brewery near the
Thames River in Chiswick since
1845. Brewing on the site,
however, goes back 350 years.
Despite its global prominence,
Fuller's retains a small company
spirit and formidably energetic
outlook. Its beers have received
countless awards, notably the
Campaign For Real Ale
Champion Beer of Britain,
which it has won five times.

London Pride

BITTER 4.1% ABV
A fruity sweet malt nose and a floral
spiced hop presence with marmalade
undercurrents.

ESB

EXTRA SPECIAL BITTER 5.5% ABV
Complex aromas, with the house-style
orange fruit complementing tangy hops
and roasted malt.

Fürstlichen Ellingen

Schloss-Strasse 19, 91792 Ellingen,
GERMANY
www.fuerst-carl.de

Owner Carl Friedrich Fürst von Wrede is a direct descendant of Napoleon's field marshal Carl Philipp, Prince of Wrede. The brewery opposite his castle in Ellingen was founded in 1690, but the brewing history of Ellingen is certainly older. The beer has been called Fürst Carl for about 200 years.

Fürst Carl Josefi Bock
BOCK 7% ABV
A creamy, malty, and full-bodied beer, with a velvet and silky texture.

Fürst Carl Urhell
LAGER 4.6% ABV
The clear yellow color is typical for a lager; the taste is pleasant and not too dry, with very little sweetness.

Galbraith's

2 Mt. Eden Road, Mt. Eden,
Auckland, **NEW ZEALAND**
www.alehouse.co.nz

Located in a former library, New
Zealand's first real ale brewpub is
best known for its home-brewed
English style ales—all served by
hand pump. Visitors can also
enjoy an excellent Abbey-style ale
and a couple of flavorsome lagers,
as well as a fine range of imports
and craft beers from other New
Zealand brewers.

Bellringers Bitter

ENGLISH BEST BITTER **4.5%** ABV
Copper colored ale with a biscuity,
toffeelike palate, plenty of earthy hops,
and an appetizingly dry finish.

Bob Hudson's Bitter

ENGLISH BITTER **4%** ABV
A full-flavored session bitter very much in
the vein of the English pale ale Timothy
Taylor's Landlord.

Gayant

63 Faubourg de Paris,
59500 Douai, **FRANCE**
www.brasseurs-gayant.com

Established in 1919, this
independent, family-owned
brewery has always embraced
and pioneered new styles of
brewing, from ales made
using the top-fermentation
technique, to Celta, the first
non-alcoholic beer.

BREWING SECRET Brasseurs de Gayant
brews the strongest beer in France, called
Bière du Démon (12% ABV).

La Goudale
ALE 7.2% ABV

Golden, dense, and full of malty aromas,
with a slight bitterness imbued by the
Flemish hops.

Amadeus
WHEAT BEER 4.5% ABV

Cloudy and pale yellow, this is a light and
refreshing beer, with aromas of citrus
fruit and coriander.

Gilde

Hildesheimer Str. 132,
Hanover, **GERMANY**
www.gildebrau.de

It was about 500 years ago that
Cord Broyhan presented his beer
to the people of Hanover.
Broyhan—a pale style of wheat
beer—was popular for centuries
in the city. Gilde, Hanover's
longest-surviving brewery,
now owned by InBev, was
founded in 1870.

BREWING SECRET A modern version
of broyhan is exported to the US.

Ratskeller Premium Pils
PILSNER **4.9**% ABV
A dry, golden-yellow pilsner; full-bodied,
typical bitterness of hops, and a
nice finish.

Lindener Special
EXPORT **5.1**% ABV
The most successful export beer of
Niedersachsen has a golden color and
tastes pleasant with smooth yeast-flower
flavors in the mouth.

Goose Island

1800 West Fulton Street
CHICAGO, IL 60612, **USA**
www.gooseisland.com

This brewery's extensive range reflects the MBA (Master of Beer Appreciation) Program that it established shortly after opening as a brewpub in 1988. When Goose Island built its production brewery in 1995, brewmaster Greg Hall would launch dozens of styles during the course of a year. Goose Island still operates the original pub on Clybourn as well as another near Wrigley Field, and both still offer an "MBA" (actually a kind of loyalty card!).

India Pale Ale

INDIA PALE ALE 5.9% ABV
Pineapple and grapefruit, full of hop flavor, with a fruit and malt back-bone balancing the bitterness.

312 Urban Wheat

US WHEAT BEER 4.2% ABV
Typically unfiltered and hazy, with a citrussy, almost sweet, hop nose that announces it is American. Tart, fruity, with underlying creaminess.

Gourmet-bryggeriet

Bytoften 10-12,
DK-4000 Roskilde, **DENMARK**
www.gourmetbryggeriet.dk

One of the largest microbreweries in Denmark, "The Gourmet Brewery" creates specialty beers that are designed to be paired with food. The brewery's partner is a trained chef who works together with a local restaurant to create recipes that are attached to 66cl bottles for sharing. The company recently acquired the Ølfabrikken Brewery.

Ølfabrikken Porter
PORTER 7.5% ABV
Black as the night, with a thick head of foam. Intense body with coffee, chocolate, and liquorice notes.

Gourmetbryggeriet Bock
DOPPELBOCK 7.2% ABV
Deep reddish in color, with a heavy aroma of malt and caramel backing up the strong body.

Great Divide

2201 Arapahoe Street
Denver, CO 80205, **USA**
www.greatdivide.com

Opened in 1994, Great Divide
Brewing quickly earned a
reputation for carefully balanced
beers. Its ales have grown bigger
(in strength and hop character),
and the brewery's reputation has
grown, but its beers still retain
that delicate equilibrium. The
brewery is a short walk from
Coors Field, home of the Rockies
baseball team.

Hibernation Ale

OLD ALE **8.1**% ABV

A complex, earthy nose packed with
chocolate, roasted nuts, and freshly
baked molasses cookies—flavors just
keep emerging.

Titan IPA

INDIA PALE ALE **6.8**% ABV

Balanced, in a big way, with plenty of
caramel-sweet body to match the piney,
grapefruity hops throughout.

Great Lakes

2516 Market Avenue
Cleveland, OH 44113, **USA**
www.greatlakesbrewing.com

Selling its beer across a growing
region, this brewery has been an
industry leader in tracking the
quality of its beer on retailers'
shelves. Its brewing complex
always merits a visit. The original
1988 brewpub sits across from
the production brewery, which
came online in 1998. Visitors are
directed to the taproom's striking
Tiger Mahogany bar and shown
bullet holes reputedly made by
Eliot Ness, the "untouchable"
Prohibition agent who brought
down gangster Al Capone.

Edmund Fitzgerald Porter

PORTER 5.8% ABV
Perfectly balanced, chocolate-mocha
throughout, delightful fresh quality,
and a dry coffee finish.

Eliot Ness

VIENNA LAGER 6.2% ABV
Bold and hoppy in the Vienna style,
with creamy, nutty maltiness and
brisk hoppiness nicely balanced.

Green Flash

1430 Vantage Court
Vista, CA 92081, **USA**
www.greenflashbrew.com

Green Flash refers to a rare light phenomenon that lasts only seconds at sunrise or sunset over water. Green seems appropriate for a brewery gaining a national reputation for its hop-accented beers, although brewer Chuck Silva has proved adept at a wide range of styles.

West Coast IPA

INDIA PALE ALE 7% ABV
Northwest hops balanced on a solid malt base. Earthy, floral, citrussy, piney, grapefruity, and bitter.

Nut Brown Ale

BROWN ALE 5.5% ABV
Deep brown, with nuts and cocoa from the outset, and more chocolate and caramel on the palate. Subdued, earthy hops.

Greene King

Bury St. Edmunds, Suffolk,
IP33 1QT **ENGLAND**
www.greeneking.co.uk

After more than 200 years,
Greene King has developed into a
formidable and dynamic force in
the British brewing industry.
Benjamin Greene opened his
brewery in 1799 and it merged
with the rival King Brewery in
1887. The company has in recent
years acquired several of its
competitors—namely, Morland,
Ruddles, Ridley's, and Hardy &
Hanson—and closed them amid
some controversy. Belhaven of
Dunbar was another recent
acquisition, it being bought
up in 2005.

Abbot Ale

STRONG BITTER 5% ABV
A biscuit malt and spicy hop aroma, with a
tangy and bittersweet fruit and malt palate.

IPA

INDIA PALE ALE 3.6% ABV
Distinctly copper-colored, with
a clean, fresh hop savoriness and subtle,
sweetish malty nose.

Grünbach

Kellerberg 2, 85461 Bockhorn,
GERMANY
www.schlossbrauerei-gruenbach.de

Grünbach has had a host of
owners, including the famous
Paulaner and Erdinger
breweries. Alexander Noll
is currently at the helm.

BREWING SECRET Grünbach's Benno
Scharl wheat beer carries the name of an
18th-century Bavarian master brewer who
wrote an influential textbook on brewing
techniques.

Altweizen Gold
WHEAT BEER 5.3% ABV
Clear golden and finely balanced between
yeast and carbonic acid, with a lightly
sparkling, dry freshness.

Benno Scharl
WHEAT BEER 5.3% ABV
Yellow, and clouded with yeast, Benno
Scharl tastes mild and sweet, pleasant
and well balanced.

Guinness

St. James's Gate, Dublin 8,
IRELAND
www.guinness.com

When you can make a virtue out of the time it takes to pour a pint—119.5 seconds to be precise—you know you have no ordinary beer in your hands. Guinness defines stout, Ireland, and Irishness, but it is also inextricably linked with innovation in physics, chemistry, packaging, and advertising. 250 years after young Arthur Guinness's first mash, it is brewed in 50 countries worldwide and enjoyed in 150.

Guinness Original
STOUT 4.2% ABV
The packaged version's coffee and cream aroma highlights fruit, chocolate, and some late hoppiness.

Foreign Extra Stout
SPECIAL STOUT 7.5% ABV
Leafy hop aroma, with burnt toast, rich malt, bitter coffee, and liquorice flavors ripening effortlessly.

Haake-Beck

Am Deich 18/19, 28365
Bremen, **GERMANY**
www.haake-beck.de

Founded in 1826, the Haake-Beck brewery is one of the most famous in northern Germany. Milestones in the company's history include the creation of Haake-Beck Kräusen Pils and the first Maibock in 1950. It is part of the InBev stable today.

BREWING SECRET Haake-Beck's sister is the famous Beck's label, which is exported by InBev around the world.

Haake-Beck 12
EXPORT 5% ABV
This is a new Haake-Beck. A harmonious, golden beer, with a level of sweetness that is often liked by women drinkers.

Edel Hell
LAGER 4.7% ABV
A mild alternative to the pilsner: not so dry, a little bit sweet, and golden like a typical lager.

Haandbryggeriet

Thornegaten 39,
N-3015 Drammen, **NORWAY**
www.haandbryggeriet.net

This small brewery is known
for its hand-made brews and for
keeping Norwegian brewing
traditions alive. Housed in a
200-year-old wooden building,
it is run by volunteers, and
experimentation is encouraged.

BREWING SECRET As well as using old
oak wine barrels, they are now ageing
beer in former Akevitt spirit casks.

Dark Force
WHEAT STOUT 9% ABV
Uses wheat and dark roasted malts and
house wheat yeast. High hop aroma and
ample bitterness.

Norwegian Wood
TRADITIONAL ALE 6.5% ABV
Made from naturally smoked Munich,
Crystal, and chocolate malts; spiced
with locally gathered juniper twigs
and berries.

Hakusekikan

5251-1 Hirukawa Tahara,
Nagatsugawa, Gifu 509-8301, **JAPAN**
www.hakusekikan-beer.jp

One of Japan's most distinctive breweries, Hakusekikan pushes the envelope of possible beer styles. Head brewer Satoshi Niwa is brilliant and imaginative, experimenting with wild beers using airborne yeast, while also making use of long fermentation times, barrel ageing, and other methods to produce truly distinctive beers.

Super Vintage
STRONG ALE 14.3% ABV
Astonishingly fruity and complex beer, yet boasts a surprisingly dry finish. Permanently on tap at Beer Club Popeye in Tokyo.

Smoked Pale Ale
PALE ALE 5% ABV
A session pale ale given just a hint of smoked malt, with the smoky flavor appearing only in the finish.

Hambleton

Holme-on-Swale, North Yorkshire,
YO7 4JE **ENGLAND**
www.hambletonales.co.uk

A million-pound investment has
resulted in a completely new
brewery for Hambleton, with
state-of-the-art bottling facilities.
Innovation has been at the heart
of the operation since 1991, as
evident in the label designs and
bespoke brewing equipment.
Several awards, including one
for a gluten-free range, have
been well deserved.

Stallion
BITTER 4.2% ABV
For some, a true Yorkshire bitter, with its
malty character, nuttiness, and enhanced
hopping rate.

Nightmare
PORTER 5% ABV
An extra-stout porter that uses a
combination of four malts for a
massively complex flavor.

Harviestoun

Alva, Clackmannanshire,
FK12 5DQ **SCOTLAND**
www.harviestoun-brewery.co.uk

The brewers of Harviestoun say
they can't pretend it's a job—it's
their work, but also their play
and their passion. Curiosity
toward flavors and aromas wrung
from natural ingredients was the
brewery's mission in 1985, when
the business was originally set
up, and a move to a purpose-built
plant with fresh investment has
resulted in national accolades.

Bitter & Twisted

BITTER 4.2% ABV

Ripe grapefruit and lemon-influenced
hop aromas are anchored by a
distinct maltiness.

Schiehallion

PREMIUM LAGER 4.8% ABV

Cask lager, brewed with Bavarian hops
for a delightful nose. A rigid maltiness
prevails throughout.

Hawkshead

Staveley, Cumbria,
LA8 9LR **ENGLAND**
www.hawksheadbrewery.co.uk

The focus at Hawkshead is on traditional beer styles that have been given a modern twist. A new 20-barrel (3,200-liter) brewhouse was fitted out in 2006—an integral feature is a farm gate for leaning on contemplatively. The brewery's public beer hall, where award-winning ales are served, is a magnificent showcase for the beers and their provenance.

Hawkshead Red

RED ALE **4.2**% ABV
A bittersweet red ale, malty and spicy on the palate, with juicy, woody aromas.

Hawkshead Gold

BEST BITTER **4.4**% ABV
Hoppy and uncompromisingly bitter, with complex fruit flavors from its English and American hop blend.

High Falls

445 St. Paul Street
Rochester, NY 14605, **USA**
www.highfalls.com

High Falls is still brewing old-style Genesee beers on the site where they have been made since 1878. It also makes the J.W. Dundee family of beers for the traditional ale market.

BREWING SECRET High Falls is one of the largest and oldest continuously operating breweries in the US.

Genesee Cream Ale
CREAM ALE **4.9**% ABV
Pale, faintly sweet, with roast corn flavors; smooth and easy to drink.

JW Dundee's IPA
INDIA PALE ALE **6.3**% ABV
A seasonal summer beer. Relatively sweet caramel character, with more bitterness than flavor from its hops. Crisp finish.

Hite

640, Yeongdeungpo-Dong,
Yeongdeungpo, Seoul,
SOUTH KOREA
www.hite.com

Founded in 1933 as Chosun
Breweries, Hite is Korea's
leading brewer, with 60 percent
of local sales. Carlsberg is a
substantial investor in the
brewery. The present production
at Hite amounts to approximately
150 million gallons (seven
million hectoliters) per annum.
The company also makes a
rice-based wine.

Hite
LAGER 4.5% ABV
Golden in color, Hite is a light,
easy drinking beer—with an aroma
of bubblegum.

Prime Max
LAGER 4.5% ABV
Pale orange in color; with a sweetcorn
aroma, it has hints of biscuit and
citrus fruits.

Hoegaarden

Stoopkensstraat 46,
B3320 Hoegaarden, **BELGIUM**
www.inbev.com

Although this is now a brand in the portfolio of brewing giant InBev, it is the lifeblood and spirit of Pierre Celis, Belgium's preeminent brewing revolutionary, that still haunts this brewery. Proof of this came in 2007, when InBev's moguls wanted to close the plant: fate, however, obliged them to reverse their decision.

Hoegaarden Wit

WITBIER 4.9% ABV

From as early as the 18th century, the town of Hoegaarden was importing blue Curaçao oranges. The peel was mixed with coriander seeds, and, as the rich soil of the area yielded lots of wheat, a very distinct, fruity, and spicy style of beer evolved.

Hofbräu München

Hofbräuallee 1,
81829 München, **GERMANY**
www.hofbraeuhaus.com

The Hofbräuhaus in Munich is a very famous restaurant, frequented by visitors from around the world. It was founded in 1607 by Maximilian I, Duke of Bavaria. The linked brewery is situated in Riem, outside of the city.

BREWING SECRET The water used to brew Hofbräu is drawn from a depth of 490 ft (150 m).

Hofbräu Original
MÜNCHNER HELLES 5.1% ABV
This clear golden beer is refreshing and dry, with a harmonious balance of malt and hops.

Hofbräu Dunkel
DUNKEL 5.5% ABV
This is the oldest type of Bavarian beer, dark amber in color, and full of fine flavor and enticing malt aromas.

Holt

Cheetham, Manchester,
M3 1JD **ENGLAND**
www.joseph-holt.com

A family business survivor in an increasingly corporate sector, Holt's admits—with some pride—to being unashamedly old-fashioned. That does not mean backward-looking, however, and its well-structured projects and clear vision have brought steady expansion to the brewery and to its portfolio of 127 pubs.

Holt 1849

BEST BITTER 4.5% ABV
A 150-year anniversary ale, with a vibrant and generous celebratory hop flavor to match.

Holt Bitter

BITTER 4% ABV
Spicy hops dominate the aroma with tart fruitiness tempered by biscuit malt and bittersweet fruit.

Hook Norton

Banbury, Oxfordshire,
OX15 5NY **ENGLAND**
www.hooky.co.uk

A particularly striking example of a Victorian tower brewery, Hook Norton is partly powered by steam, via a series of belts, cogs, and shafts. Drays pulled by shire horses deliver to local pubs, further demonstrating how the brewery likes to preserve traditional practices. While doing this, Hook Norton also produces some of the country's most outstanding ales.

Old Hooky
STRONG BITTER **4.6**% ABV
Beautifully poised, with a piquant, fruity nature and malt character rounding off a bitter finish.

Hooky Bitter
BITTER **3.6**% ABV
Subtly hoppy on the nose, then malt and fruit appear, before a returning hop finish.

COTSWOLDS, ENGLAND

The village of Hook Norton in north Oxfordshire is the perfect base for any visitor exploring the Cotswolds or the city of Oxford. For the traveler, three of the village's pubs—the Sun, the Pear Tree, and the Gate Hangs High—all offer accommodation.

1 DAY 1: **HOOK NORTON BREWERY**
This is a near-perfect example of a Victorian tower brewery. It is still powered by a steam engine, and the making of Hook Norton's beers is a tactile, aural, and visual experience. Only the finest malted barley is used in the mash tun, and this needs to be manually removed when the wort is drained off the grist. The seemingly magical transformation of turning sweet wort into alcohol takes place in the brewery's hard-working open fermenters. A horse-drawn dray still delivers beer to local pubs. The Visitor Center is open from Monday to Saturday, though tours of the brewery must be booked beforehand via the website. The tour is followed by some sampling of Hook Norton beer. *Brewery Lane, Hook Norton (www.hooky.co.uk)*

2 DAY 2: **WYCHWOOD BREWERY**
The drive from Hook Norton to Witney takes in some glorious countryside, and at the end of the trip is the Wychwood Brewery. Tours of the brewery can be booked online. They last for two hours and go through the brewing process for Wychwood and Brakspear beers, from raw ingredients to the finished product. The tour takes in Brakspear's famous "Double Drop system" fermenting vessels. *Eagle Maltings, The Crofts, Witney (www.wychwood.co.uk)*

3 **THE KING'S HEAD INN**
Before returning to Hook Norton, pass by Cotswold Brewing (www.cotswoldbrewing company.com) at Foscot. Unusually for a British micro, brewer Richard Keene makes continental-style lagers. With a meandering stream at its side, the King's Head Inn, at nearby Bledington, is the perfect place to drink a glass of Cotswold Brewing's beer. *The King's Head Inn, The Green, Bledington (www.thekingsheadinn.net)*

TRAIL OR TOUR STATS
3 days
100 miles (160 km)

0m   5 miles

0km   10km

Hook Norton **1**

START

A3400   A361   Deddington   M40

Great Tew

Chipping Norton

O X F O R D S H I R E

Stow-on-the-Wold

Enstone

Bledington

A4260

3

A44

A361   River Evenlode

A4095

Charlbury   Wootton   Kirtlington

A424

Shipton under Wychwood

Woodstock

A34

A4095   Kidlington

Burford   **2**

Witney

A40   A40

Eynsham

A34

FINISH   **4**

A420   **Oxford**

---

4 DAY 3: **OXFORD**
The third day of the trail offers a chance to sample some of the fabulous pubs in the historical city of Oxford—a place where good beer, culture, and a convivial atmosphere sit cosily together.

The Bear
Small and friendly, The Bear is on a narrow lane between Christ Church and Oriel colleges. It claims to be the oldest pub in Oxford, and is built on the site of a former bear-fighting pit. The walls are decorated by a collection of 5,000 ties. *6 Alfred Street, Oxford*

King's Arms
The King's Arms sits at the end of Broad Street, which is famous for its colleges and bookshops. The large pub is a warren of rooms and is much loved by locals and students. *40 Holywell Street, Oxford*

Turf Tavern
Hard to find but worth the search, the Turf Tavern is built on the only remaining part of the city wall. It sells a fabulous collection of British beers. *Bath Place, Holywell, Oxford; for directions go to the pub's website: www.theturftavern.co.uk*

Eagle & Child
Near Oxford's dreaming spires and the Ashmolean museum of art and architecture, the Eagle & Child was a haunt of writers J.R.R. Tolkein and C.S. Lewis, who were part of a literary group in the 1930s and 40s called the *Inklings*. *49 St. Giles, Oxford*

Hue

243 Nguyen Sinh Cung
Hue City, **VIETNAM**

The Hue Brewery is based in Hue City, the old capital of Vietnam, on the banks of the famous Perfume River in central Vietnam. Carlsberg—which entered Vietnam in 1993 with the acquisition of a 60 percent stake in South East Asia Brewery, based in the north of the country—now has a 50 percent share in the Hue Brewery.

Hue

LAGER 5% ABV

A yellow corn color with a thin white head, and the body seems somewhat thin too. It is an easy-drinking beer, without surprises and a nose with hints of toast. Not much complexity, but a refresher nonetheless.

Huvila

Puistokatu 4, FI-57100,
Savonlinna, **FINLAND**
www.panimoravintolahuvila.fi

This craft brewery, making British-style ales, *sideri* (cider), and *sahti*, is located in Savonlinna, a popular tourist area in the Lake Saimaa area. The complex offers good food at the brewery-restaurant Huvila, bed and breakfast, live music, brewery tours, and a brewing school.

BREWING SECRET All of Huvila's products are unfiltered.

Huvila Porter
PORTER 5.5% ABV
English roasted malts give a strong coffeelike, roasted aroma with a hint of chocolate.

Huvila ESB
STRONG BITTER 5.2% ABV
Robustly hopped with a fruity and floral aroma, complex flavors, and a long and bitter aftertaste.

Jämtlands Bryggeri

Box 224, SE-831 23 Östersund,
SWEDEN
www.jamtlandsbryggeri.se

This innovative small microbrewery was established in 1996 in the capital of the Jämtland region of central Sweden. It brews a wide variety of beer, including a strong English ale, Baltic Porter, and Vienna lager. It consistently wins awards at the Stockholm Beer Festival.

BREWING SECRETS It draws from British, German, and Alsace beer styles.

President
PORTER 4.8% ABV
This bottom-fermented beer has a medium bitterness and the soft aroma of Czech Saaz hops.

Oatmeal Porter
PORTER 4.7% ABV
An unfiltered and top-fermented porter with a ruby-black color. Espresso in a glass!

Jandelsbrunner

Hauptstr. 17, 94118 Jandelsbrunn,
GERMANY
www.jandelsbrunner.de

The Langs have owned this
brewery since 1810. In the 20th
century, there was renewal of
equipment such as new filling
machines, and the construction
of new production plants and
maturing cellars.

BREWING SECRET In 2004 photovoltaic
equipment was added, to harness the
power of the sun for brewing.

Doppelbock

DOPPELBOCK 8% ABV
The color of this doppelbock is
mahogany, the taste malty, flowery,
and slightly sweet, with a nice bitter
note when finishing.

Ur-Weizen

WHEAT BEER 5.3% ABV
Amber-colored and cloudy from the yeast,
this malty beer tastes flowery with a mild,
sweet finish.

Jolly Pumpkin

3115 Broad Street
Dexter, MI 48130, **USA**
www.jollypumpkin.com

Not quite like any other brewery in the US, Jolly Pumpkin Artisan Ales allows its beers to develop under the influence of local wild yeast. All beers are aged in barrels, and are often blended and re-fermentated in the bottle to deliver effervescent beer. Though its output is small, the brewery has developed a national following.

Oro de Calabaza

BELGIAN STRONG GOLDEN ALE 8% ABV
Golden and cloudy, tart and spicy, with orchard fruit and citrus. Develops with age.

Bam Biere

SAISON 4.5% ABV
The whole exceeds the sum of its parts in this "farmhouse" ale, from the hops (billowing head, dry finish) to the spicy malts.

Jopen

Minckelersweg 2a,
2031 EM Haarlem, **NETHERLANDS**
www.jopen.nl

Jopen was founded in 1995 with the intention of recreating old beer styles specifically from the Haarlem locale— once an important brewing center. This is Holland's only brewery to concentrate on local recipes, and no other in the world produces beer in these styles. A brewpub to showcase the beers is due to open soon.

Jopen Koyt
GRUIT BEER 8.5% ABV
A recreation of a pre-hop beer brewed from three grains and herbs. Fruity, spicy, and delicious.

Jopen Hoppenbier
AMBER ALE 6.5% ABV
Based on a recipe from 1501 using barley, wheat, and oats; hints of coriander, ginger, and cloves complement spicy hops.

Kelham Island

Sheffield, South Yorkshire,
S3 8SA **ENGLAND**
www.kelhambrewery.co.uk

Since Kelham Island opened in
1990, Sheffield's four large
breweries have closed down,
which makes Kelham's success
all the more remarkable. An
astonishing range of awards has
been collected along the way.

BREWING SECRET Pale Rider and Easy
Rider both make great use of highly
fragrant American hops.

Pale Rider
STRONG BITTER 5.2% ABV
Strong but delicately fruity multi-award
winner, which profits from an
adventurous use of American hops.

Easy Rider
BITTER 4.3% ABV
A subtle pale ale, its initial crisp
bitterness surrendering only to a
lingering fruity palate.

Keo

Franklin Roosevelt Ave, Limassol,
3602 **CYPRUS**
www.keogroup.com

Limassol is the main port and
fastest-growing city on the island
of Cyprus. It is also home to the
Keo Brewery, and no trip to
Limassol is complete without
visiting the plant, which lies just
beyond the Old Port. During
the week, there is a daily tour
around the brewery—finishing,
of course, in the tasting room.

Keo
LAGER 4.5% ABV
A pale lager with a thick head and a sweet
malt taste, it is easy on the palate and
very drinkable.

Five Beer
LAGER 5% ABV
Deep amber in color, it is rich in malt and
low in bitterness. Sweet in the finish.

Klein Duimpje

Parallelweg 2, 2182 CP Hillegom,
NETHERLANDS
www.kleinduimpje.nl

This is the brewery of a prize-winning amateur brewer, Erik Bouman, whose porter was chosen as the best of more than 400 entries at the Dutch Homebrewing Championship of 1997. Bouman's competition success prompted him to start brewing professionally.
His extensive range of top-fermenting ales includes his celebrated porter.

Hillegoms Tarwe Bier
WITBIER 5.5% ABV
Flavored with coriander and orange peel, this wheat beer is spicy, citric, and just ever so slightly sweet.

Porter
PORTER 5.5% ABV
Espressolike roast malt combines with a chocolate sweetness, backed up with liquorice and toast.

Kona

75-5629 Kuakini Highway
Kailua Kona, HI 97640, **USA**
www.konabrewingco.com

Sales are booming everywhere
for Kona Brewing, which offers
mainland drinkers "a pint of
paradise." The Big Island
brewery added capacity to meet
growing demand in Hawaii,
while sales in 17 mainland states
have increased even faster. Beers
sold on the mainland are made
under contract at Widmer
Brothers in Oregon.

Pipeline Porter
PORTER **5.4**% ABV
Brewed with local Kona coffee, its flavor
is well-integrated. Roasty malt, oily, with
chocolate notes.

Fire Rock Pale Ale
PALE ALE **6**% ABV
Reddish-orange with slightly sweet
caramel aromas and flavor, spicy
and citric hops are cleverly integrated
and balanced.

König Ludwig

Augsburger Stre. 41, 82256
Fürstenfeldbruck, **GERMANY**
www.kaltenberg.de

The history of the Bavarian royal
family, the Wittelsbachers, is
closely connected with the art of
beermaking. Today, HRH
Luitpold Prince of Bavaria
continues the family business
successfully with his brands
König Ludwig and Kaltenberg.
The latter brand name refers to
the brewery at Kaltenberg Castle.

König Ludwig Dunkel

DUNKEL 5.1% ABV

Amber, with a smooth taste of dark malt
and fine hops, this is the most popular
dunkel in Germany.

König Ludwig Weissbier

WHEAT BEER 5.5% ABV

One of the most popular wheat beers
in Bavaria; cloudy yellow, with fine hops
in the finish. A very traditional, non-
filtered specialty.

De Koninck

Mechelse Steenweg 291,
B2018 Antwerpen, **BELGIUM**
www.dekoninck.be

De Koninck is an icon—as is its
main beer. It embodies the town
of Antwerp—whose inhabitants
are a proud lot, and will say so.
The amber "bolleke" (actually
the glass) is still the staple diet
in many bars.

BREWING SECRET The draft version
is unpasteurized and should be tried
at its source.

De Koninck
AMBER "SPECIALE BELGE" 5% ABV
Amber malts, residual sugars, and hops
give excellent balance to a fine ale, with
a slight but distinct sulfury aroma and
biscuit character. The draft version
is particularly good—available in cask
in the UK as well.

Kuhnhenn

5919 Chicago Road
Warren, MI 48092, **USA**
www.kbrewery.com

Brothers Brett and Eric
Kuhnhenn turned the hardware
store their father ran for 35 years
into a small brewery, winery,
meadery, and brew-on-premises
(where customers can make their
own beer). The national
reputation of Kuhnhenn shows
how word of mouth—and the
Internet—can help small
breweries develop
a cult following.

Raspberry Eisbock
EISBOCK 10.6% ABV
A small-run beer. Complex, rich with
raspberries, chocolate, warming alcohol,
and a closing tartness.

Penetration Porter
PORTER 5.9% ABV
Almost black, with roasted coffee,
chocolate, and dark fruits like cherry
filling the nose and the mouth. Citrussy
hop finish.

Kulmbacher

Lichtenfelser Str. 9, 95326
Kulmbach, **GERMANY**
www.kulmbacher.de

The name of Kulmbach, a city
in northern Bavaria, is known to
beer-lovers throughout the world.
Its fame began with the offerings
of beer master Wolfgang Reichel
in 1846. Since his time, many
other brands have joined the
company, and production is now
about 70 million gallons (300
million liters) of beer each year.

Mönchshof Schwarzbier
SCHWARZBIER **4.9%** ABV

Dark roasted malts and fine hops.
The deep, dark color and fine aroma
are typical of schwarzbiers.

Kapuziner Weissbier
WHEAT BEER **5.4%** ABV

Naturally cloudy, sparkling and with
a sweet and fruity taste; this unfiltered
beer is typical of the wheat beer style.

Lambrate

Via Adelchi 5, 20131 Milano, **ITALY**
www.birrificiolambrate.com

The first (and still the best) brewpub in Milan, founded in 1996 by brothers Davide and Giampaolo Sangiorgi and their friend Fabio Brocca after a visit to 't IJ Brewery in Amsterdam. They have recently expanded production, adding some new, interesting ales. The menu features some creative beer-influenced dishes, such as pork cooked in beer mash.

Ghisa
SMOKED ALE 5% ABV
Ebony in color with a "cappuccino" foam; lighty smoked, easy to drink, and balanced, with plum notes and a long, hoppy finish.

Montestella
BLOND ALE 4.9% ABV
Their flagship ale; pale, with fresh aromas of hay and hops with a long, dry finish cleansing the palate.

Lao Brewery

Km 12 Thadeua Road,
Vientiane, **LAOS**
www.beer-lao.com

The Lao Brewery began
production in 1973 and was
originally known as Brasseries
et Glaci è res du Laos. Two years
later, in 1975, it became state
owned. In 2002, Carlsberg and
TCC, a Thai company, each
agreed to acquire a 25 percent
stake in Lao Brewery; the
remaining shares are still held
by the Laos government.

Beerlao
LAGER 5% ABV
Described as Asia's best beer, Beerlao
has a pleasant sweetness. Light
bitterness, with hints of honey.

Beerlao Dark
LAGER 6.5% ABV
Reddish brown, it is full of sweet
toffee and toast flavors. A short but
warming finish.

Left Hand

1265 Boston Avenue
Longmont, CO 80501, **USA**
www.lefthandbrewing.com

The company takes its name from the Arapahoe Chief Niwot, his name translating as "left hand." Originally brewing English-style ales, the brewery merged in 1998 with Tabernash, known for Bavarian-inspired beers. Those beers have now been phased out, but Left Hand continues to develop a wide range of beer styles and produces many seasonal brews too.

Milk Stout

MILK STOUT **5.3**% ABV
Complex and smooth, chocolate and burnt toast in the aroma and flavor constantly balanced by creamy sweetness.

Blackjack Porter

PORTER **5.2**% ABV
Chocolate and liquorice aromas, medium body, with hints of dark cherries and a smooth, dry finish.

Leinenkugel's

1 Jefferson Avenue
Chippewa Falls, WI 54729, **USA**
www.leinie.com

Since 1988, when Miller
Brewing bought a controlling
interest, the Jacob Leinenkugel
Brewing Company has grown
into one of the largest regional
breweries in the country,
distributing in almost
every state.

BREWING SECRET The brewery,
founded in 1867, still offers a range
reflecting its German heritage.

Creamy Dark
US DARK LAGER **4.9**% ABV
As creamy as promised, chocolate with
coffee and cream character and a dryish
not-too-bitter finish.

Sunset Wheat
US WHEAT BEER **4.9**% ABV
Light but complex beer, almost a fruit
salad of aromas and flavors, with some
wheaty tartness and coriander spiciness.

Lion

700 North Pennsylvania Avenue
Wilkes-Barre, PA 18705, **USA**
www.lionbrewery.com

The Lion Brewery, founded in
1905, is a survivor—the last of
dozens of breweries that once
operated in northeastern
Pennsylvania. Most recently the
brewery has emphasized this
heritage with its Stegmaier
brand of good-value traditional
beers, the roots of which go back
to 1857.

Steg 150

VIENNA LAGER **5.5%** ABV
Created to celebrate the brewery's 150th
anniversary. Smells like warm toast,
malt-accented, lightly sweet but smooth,
not cloying.

Stegmaier Porter

PORTER **5.5%** ABV
Notes of sweet chocolate and ripe fruit
matched with toasty malt and a coffee-
bitter finish.

Lion Brewery

254 Colombo Road, Biyagama,
SRI LANKA
www.lionbeer.com

The company's best-known beer
is the bottle conditioned Lion
Stout. The beer is brewed from
British, Czech, and Danish malts,
with Styrian hops and an English
yeast strain. All the ingredients
are transported along precarious
roads to the brewery, located
3,500 ft (1,000 m) above sea level
in the midst of tea plantations.

Lion Stout

STOUT 8% ABV

A world-class beer, with pruney, mocha
aromas and flavors. It has a tarlike
oiliness of body and a peppery, bitter-
chocolate finish. The alcohol gives it
a long warming finish.

Little Creatures

40 Mews Road, Fremantle,
Western Australia 6160,
AUSTRALIA
www.littlecreatures.com.au

Based in an enormous hangarlike building on the water's edge at Fremantle, Little Creatures combines a bar/restaurant within a busy microbrewery. The flagship Pale Ale is inspired by the likes of the US-based Sierra Nevada, and, along with the venue, has been a runaway success. The company is currently gearing up production, and has announced bold plans for themed bars in Sydney and Melbourne, and a second brewery to be built in Victoria.

Little Creatures Pale Ale
US PALE ALE 5.2% ABV
Citrus/grapefruit hop aromatics; chewy malt and citrus-tinged, robust bitterness.

Rogers' Beer
AMBER ALE 3.8% ABV
Biscuity malt notes; caramel-laced mid-palate and spicy-citrus hoppiness; short finish.

Locher

Industriestrasse 12, CH - 9050
Appenzell, **SWITZERLAND**
www.appenzellerbier.ch

Appenzell is Switzerland's
smallest province (kanton), but
the beer produced by the local
brewery has won it a lot of fame.

BREWING SECRET In the 1990s, the
Locher family found out that beers
brewed on the full moon ferment more
easily; they have, therefore, created a line
of "Vollmond-brews."

Vollmond
ORGANIC LAGER 5.2% ABV
An aroma of hops and lemon zest;
medium body—chewy; hoppy, but not
excessively bitter.

Holzfass-Bier
LAGER 5.2% ABV
Aromas of sweetcorn, very little
carbonation, and a distinctive note from
the oak in which it is matured.

Löwenbräu

Nymphenburger Str. 7, 80335
München, **GERMANY**
www.loewenbraeu.de

Löwenbräu is one of the most
famous brands in the world. The
company is more than 500 years
old. In 1948, only three years
after the end of World War II,
Löwenbräu began exporting
again: first to Switzerland, then
further afield. In 1997 there was
a marriage between Löwenbräu
and Spatenbräu; today both are
part of the global player InBev.

Löwenbräu Triumphator
DOPPELBOCK 7.6% ABV
Dark brown in color, the Triumphator has
a strong flavor of malt, but only a subtle
aroma of hops. Sweet.

Löwenbräu Urtyp
EXPORT 5.4% ABV
A balanced flavor with fine aromas of
malt; full-bodied, pleasant, and fresh,
with mild hops in the finish.

Mad River

195 Taylor Way
Blue Lake, CA 95525, **USA**
www.madriverbrewing.com

Founder Bob Smith built his brewery in 1989 using recycled materials, and has since received many awards for its waste-reduction programs. Mad River reuses 98 percent of its residuals and generates just one yard/cubic meter of waste a month while brewing about 250,000 gallons of beer per year.

Jamaica Red Ale

AMBER ALE **6.6**% ABV

First made for the annual reggae festival. Sweetish nose, with crystal malts and solid, refreshing hops.

Steelhead Scotch Porter

PORTER **6.4**% ABV

Distinctly a porter, with roasted malt and a touch of sourness. Caramel notes and hints of smoke add complexity.

Malt Shovel

99 Pyrmont Bridge Road,
Camperdown, Sydney,
New South Wales 2050, **AUSTRALIA**
www.maltshovel.com.au

Positioned as Lion Nathan's craft brewing arm, the Malt Shovel Brewery has an impressive portfolio of beer styles under brewmaster Dr. Charles "Chuck" Hahn. The brewery's first release in 1998 was Amber Ale, which found ready acceptance with traditional lager drinkers. Their James Squire brands are named after a former convict and highwayman, who became the colony's first successful hop grower and brewer.

Malt Shovel India Pale Ale
INDIA PALE ALE 5.6% ABV
Chewy, caramel-tinged maltiness balanced by robust (dry-hopped) hop flavor and lingering bitterness.

James Squire Porter
PORTER 5% ABV
Hints of coffee, dark chocolate, and dark fruit (plums); a sumptuous beer, with a smooth finish.

Marston's

Burton upon Trent, Staffordshire,
DE14 2BW **ENGLAND**
www.marstonsbeercompany.co.uk

The company operates three
sites: the Park Brewery in
Wolverhampton, which brews
Banks's, Hanson's, and Mansfield
beers; Jennings Brewery at
Cockermouth in the Lake
District, and the Albion Brewery
in Burton upon Trent.
Throughout its long existence
it has acquired several of
its competitors. Then, in 1999,
Marston's itself was taken over
by Wolverhampton & Dudley
Breweries, which changed its
name to Marston's PLC in 2007.

Pedigree
BEST BITTER 4.4% ABV
A British institution—sweetly hop-laden,
with the vague sulfur aroma that's
characteristic of Burton ales.

Old Empire
INDIA PALE ALE 5.7% ABV
A stylish India Pale Ale, with hop and
fruit flavors and a dry extra-hop finish.

Matilda Bay

130 Stirling Highway, North
Fremantle, Western Australia 6159,
AUSTRALIA
www.matildabay.com.au

Australia's first modern craft
brewery kicked off in Fremantle
in 1984, was acquired by Foster's
six years later, and has been
revitalized in recent times.
Original brews such as Redback
(a hefeweizen) and Dogbolter (a
dark lager) have been
supplemented with a wide range
of beer styles. Much of the new
direction occurred under the
watch of head brewer Brad
Rogers, who has since left the
Foster's fold after 15 years to
embark on a new brewing venture.

Dogbolter
DARK LAGER 5.2% ABV
Roasty, dark chocolate notes; complex
mid-palate; smooth, coffee-ish finish.

Bohemian Pilsner
CZECH PILSNER 5% ABV
A solid maltiness to the pilsner
is well balanced with a generous
hop bitterness.

McAuslan

5080 St-Ambroise, Montréal,
Québec, H4C 2G1, **CANADA**
www.mcauslan.com

McAuslan Brewing began in
January of 1989 when its founder
Peter McAuslan decided to turn
his home-brewing hobby into a
business. It quickly established
itself as one of the area's best
microbreweries and was one
of the first in Canada to bottle
its products. It produces a
challenging range of
seasonal beers.

St-Ambroise Apricot Ale

FRUITY WHEAT BEER 5% ABV
Apricot essence and malted wheat
combine to create an original tasting
beer with a clean, fruit nose.

St-Ambroise Oatmeal Stout

STOUT 5% ABV
Brewed from dark malts and roasted
barley, this stout carries strong espresso
and chocolate notes.

Meantime

Greenwich, London,
SE7 8RX **ENGLAND**
www.meantimebrewing.com

Preferring to be known as the brewery that can't be pigeonholed could be self-regarding, but the approach of master brewer Alastair Hook is purposeful—to demonstrate the exciting flavor potential that beer has to offer.

BREWING SECRET Research into, and recreation of, beers from the past is an abiding passion here, as exemplified by Meantime's India Pale Ale.

Meantime Chocolate

SPECIALITY STRONG BEER **6.5%** ABV
Complex malt structure, with dark chocolate releasing vanilla notes to create a rich, memorable infusion.

India Pale Ale

INDIA PALE ALE **7.5%** ABV
Massively hoppy, with herbal, spice, and grass tiers grasping the strength of the original IPAs.

Mendocino

South Highway 101
Hopland, CA 13351, **USA**
www.mendobrew.com

Mendocino Brewing was one of the first success stories among US "boutique" breweries (as they were called at the time). It opened in 1983 as the Hopland Brewery, having acquired equipment, the house yeast, and even a few employees from the groundbreaking, but by then defunct, New Albion Brewery.

Red Tail Ale

AMBER ALE **6.1**% ABV

An earthy nose includes hints of orchard fruits. Layers of creamy malt with notes of liquorice.

Blue Heron

PALE ALE **6.1**% ABV

Orange zest and lemon rind to start, giving way to traditional biscuity malt and a balanced, moderate bitterness.

Mikkeller

Slien 2, 2.tv,
DK-1766 Copenhagen, **DENMARK**
www.mikkeller.dk

An innovative brewery
producing an eclectic range
of beer. Mikkeller adopts an
American rule-breaking
approach to brewing and
has achieved significant
international recognition
with several of its brews.

BREWING SECRET The brewery
recently introduced Black, the strongest
beer ever made by a Danish brewer.

Beer Geek Breakfast

OATMEAL STOUT **7.5%** ABV
An award-winning stout with a rich nose,
smooth and balanced taste, and coffee
and chocolate notes.

Black

IMPERIAL STOUT **17.5%** ABV
Exceptional body of sugars, roasted
coffee beans, and black chocolate;
a complex and lingering aftertaste.

Minhas

1208 14th Avenue
Monroe, WI 53566, **USA**
www.minhasbrewery.com

Ravinder Minhas was just 24
years old when he bought the
historic Joseph Huber Brewery
in 2006 to produce his popular
Mountain Creek brands, already
brewed under contract in Monroe
for Canadian distribution.
Minhas Craft Brewery still makes
the Huber brands (dating back to
1843), Berghoff beers, and a line
of grocery store house label
beers as well.

Lazy Mutt

GOLDEN ALE 4.8% ABV

The first released under the Minhas
brand, billed as a "farmhouse ale" by
the brewery but more summer ale than
a *saison*.

Huber Bock

BOCK 5.4% ABV

Toasty and dry, with caramel notes. Best
at Baumgartner's Cheese Store & Tavern
near the brewery.

Minoh AJI

3-19-11 Makiochi, Minoh City, Osaka 562-0004, **JAPAN**
www.minoh-beer.jp

Established by liquor store owner Masaji Oshita, and run by his daughters Kaori and Mayuko, Minoh AJI brewery mostly makes beers based on American craft beer styles.

BREWING SECRET Among the more distinctive beers are two that contain hemp and one that uses Cabernet Sauvignon grape juice.

Minoh AJI Stout
STOUT 5.5% ABV
Brewed in the Irish style, with lots of roast flavor and creamy texture, this stout has a subdued bitterness.

Double IPA
STRONG IPA 9% ABV
Bold and exciting, this strong beer is only produced as a seasonal so far, but its popularity may lead to it becoming available year-round.

Moa

Jacksons Rd, RD3 Blenheim,
NEW ZEALAND
www.moabeer.co.nz

Nestled among vines in
Marlborough's wine country
is Moa's brewery and tasting
room—the brainchild of
winemaker Josh Scott, who
wanted to make super premium
beers with the winemaking
techniques used for Champagne-
style sparkling wines.

BREWING SECRET Moa's larger
750 ml bottles undergo the full *méthode
traditionelle* production regime.

Moa Original
BOTTLE-CONDITIONED PILS 5.5% ABV
Extended yeast contact rewards this
delightful dry, crisp pilsner with a
savory toastiness.

Moa Blanc
BOTTLE-CONDITIONED
WHEAT BEER 5.5% ABV
Dry, crisp, hints of banana and vanilla;
soft natural carbonation.

Moctezuma

Monterrey/Veracruz-Llave, **MEXICO**
www.femsa.com

Mexico's most innovative brewer, Moctezuma also has operations in Brazil and is an important exporter of beer to the US. It has a powerful brand portfolio that includes Tecate, Dos Equis, Sol, Indio, Bohemia, and Carta Blanc, many of which are sold in style bars worldwide. Its beers tend to be smooth, with a spritzy finish.

Dos Equis
VIENNA LAGER **4.8**% ABV
Rich and dark red, with chocolate orange flavors; its warming sweetness gives way to a long finish.

Sol
LAGER **4.5**% ABV
A crisp, light-bodied lager with a corn syrup aroma.

De Molen

Overtocht 43, 2411 BS Bodegraven,
NETHERLANDS
www.brouwerijdemolen.nl

Since starting Molen in 2004,
brewer Menno Olivier has
quickly gained an enviable
reputation. This is one of only
a handful of Dutch micros to
export; its cask-conditioned beer,
Engel, is designed especially for
the UK market.

BREWING SECRET Aficionados regard
Tsarina Esra, an Imperial porter, as one
of Europe's very finest beers.

Borefts Blond

BLOND ALE 6.5% ABV
Unlike many blondes, hops dominate
here. Orange, pine, resin, and grass
flavors fill the mouth.

Borefts Stout

STOUT 7% ABV
Packed with all the roasty malt flavors
you expect from a stout. Complex,
characterful, harmonious.

Biervision Monstein

Monstein, CH-7278 Davos,
SWITZERLAND
www.biervision-monstein.ch

Andreas Aegerter and Christian
Ochs started this village brewery
high up in the mountains near
Davos in 2001, along with 756
small investors (each of them
a devoted customer). They
all shared the vision that there
is a market for unusual beers,
as well as beer-related products,
such as cheese crusted with malt
and spirits distilled from beer.

Mungga

KÖLSCH **3.5**% ABV
Brewed from organic Swiss ingredients,
Mungga ("groundhog") has aromas
of violets, a dry taste, and an
elegant bitterness.

Royal 11

SPICED BEER **6.5**% ABV
Reddish, with pleasant cherry aromas
(from the local liqueur Röteli); fruity
and only faintly bitter.

Moo Brew

655 Main Road, Berriedale, Hobart,
Tasmania 7011, **AUSTRALIA**
www.moobrew.com.au

A stunningly appointed
microbrewery, with commanding
views of Derwent River and
Mount Wellington from the
second-story, glass-fronted
brewhouse. An off-shoot of
Moorilla Estate winery, Moo
Brew has set a new benchmark
among Australian craft
producers, with slick packaging,
uncompromising beers, and
premium pricing.

Moo Brew Pilsner

CZECH PILSNER 5% ABV
Bright, golden, with finely-beaded
bubbles; honey-ish malt character
balanced by herbal hop bitterness.

Moo Brew Pale Ale

US PALE ALE 4.9% ABV
Citrus aromatics; grapefruit notes
dominate mid-palate, rounded out
with substantial, tingling bitter finish.

Moorhouse's

Burnley, Lancashire,
BB11 5EN **ENGLAND**
www.moorhouses.co.uk

Mineral water and low-alcohol "hop bitters" were William Moorhouse's forte. He started his business in 1865, but his successors failed to achieve a great deal in terms of brewing beer until fresh investment in infrastructure arrived in 1988. Further improvements and additions accelerated growth and helped create the admirable reputation that Moorhouse ales have today.

Pendle Witches Brew
STRONG BITTER 5.1% ABV
Distinctive and amber-colored, the beer has a full malty palate and a resonant fruity hop finale.

Black Cat
MILD 3.4% ABV
Full, dark, and complex, with distinctive chocolate malt and liquorice flavors, and a hoppy finish.

Moosehead

89 Main Street West, Saint John,
New Brunswick, E2M 3H2, **CANADA**
www.moosehead.ca

Canada's oldest independent
brewery can trace its roots back
to 1867, when Susannah Oland
first started brewing in her
Dartmouth, Nova Scotia
backyard. Today, the company
is still owned and operated by
the Oland family. Moosehead
has stakes in McAuslan and
wholly owns the Niagara Falls
Brewing Company.

Moosehead Lager

LAGER 5% ABV
Pale, staw-colored, clean-tasting session
beer; best drunk cold.

Clancy Amber Ale

ALE 5% ABV
Top-fermented, Clancy's is a reddish
beer, with a distinct malt aroma and
overlays of caramel.

Multi Bintang

Surabaya, Central Java, **INDONESIA**
www.multibintang.co.id

Indonesia's largest brewery produces and markets a range of drinks, including Bir Bintang, Heineken, Guinness Stout, and the low alcohol Green Sands. It was founded in 1929, with Heineken taking a share of the company in the 1930s. Though taken over by the Indonesian government in 1957, Heineken became involved again in 1967, and today it is largely owned by them.

Bintang Bir Pilsener

LAGER 4.8% ABV

A fresh malty aroma gives way to a dry hoppy bitter finish—the beer clearly draws on its Dutch ancestry.

Bintang Gold

LAGER 4.8% ABV

A slightly darker variation of the pilsener, brewed to commemorate the republic's golden anniversary.

New Belgium

500 Linden Street
Fort Collins, CO 80524, **USA**
www.newbelgium.com

Jeff Lebesch and Kim Jordan
started out with a system, built
to Belgian specifications, in their
cellar in 1991. They now operate
the third largest craft brewery
in the US. Best known for Fat
Tire Ale, the brewery offers
quite a wide range of beers,
including its outstanding
Blue Paddle Pilsener.

BREWING SECRET New Belgium has
more capacity for ageing beer on wood
than any brewery other than Rodenbach
Brewery in Belgium.

Fat Tire
AMBER ALE **5.3**% ABV
Biscuity, malty nose, with toasted caramel
in the middle and a balanced finish on the
sweet side of dry.

Mothership Wit
WITBIER **4.8**% ABV
The brewery's first organic beer. Fruity
and spicy; a creamy texture and wheat
tartness on the tongue. Refreshing acidity
at the finish.

New Glarus

Highway 69
New Glarus, WI 53574, **USA**
www.newglarusbrewing.com

In 2008, New Glarus Brewing moved into a $21 million plant, just outside a picturesque village settled by Swiss pioneers in 1845. The attractive complex is designed to look like a Wisconsin dairy farm. In 2002 it was a microbrewery that made 13,700 barrels; by 2007, it had increased this fivefold. The expansion allowed the brewery to double production and keep pace with soaring sales and the demand for brewmaster Dan Carey's fruit beers and limited-edition "Unplugged" brews.

Spotted Cow

CREAM ALE 4.8% ABV

Faintly fruity, tasting of fresh peaches. Pleasantly grainy, light on the tongue, and refreshing.

Fat Squirrel

BROWN ALE 5.5%

Hazelnuts on the nose, blending with chocolate and caramel flavors; nicely balanced by earthy hops.

New Holland

690 Commerce Court
Holland, MI 49423, **USA**
www.newhollandbrew.com

New Holland Brewing bottle caps carry the slogan "Art in Fermented Form," which extends from beer to a line of brandy-flavored vodka, gin, rum, and other spirits. To keep up with demand for its assertive beers, the brewery recently put on line a used copper-domed, three-vessel brewhouse acquired from Germany.

The Poet

OATMEAL STOUT **6.5**% ABV
Abundant roast, chocolate, and dark, rummy fruits. Full-bodied and creamy enough to balance the coffee start.

Black Tulip

TRIPLE **9**% ABV
Floral, with candy and honey sweetness, and fruity notes. Sweet but tart in the mouth, accented by spicy, bitter hops.

Nils Oscar

Fruängsgatan 2,
SE-611 31 Nyköping, **SWEDEN**
www.nilsoscar.se

This microbrewery and distillery was established in 1996 and makes well-balanced beers that go well with food. It has won many awards, including four medals in the World Beer Cup.

BREWING SECRET Nils Oscar has its own maltings, and a farm where barley and other cereals for malting are grown.

Imperial Stout
IMPERIAL STOUT 7% ABV
Well balanced and rich from ageing. Chocolate aromas with caramel giving way to a bittersweet finish.

India Ale
INDIA PALE ALE 5.3% ABV
Heavily hopped with Amarillo, giving an aroma of tropical fruits; the fruitiness is balanced by the crystal malt sweetness.

Nøgne Ø

Gamle Rykene Kraftstasjon,
Lunde N-4885 Grimstad, **NORWAY**
www.nogne-o.com

Kjetil Jikiun launched Nøgne Ø
("naked island") in 2003 after
learning home-brewing in the
US. Now his brewery is Norway's
largest supplier of bottle-
conditioned ale.

BREWING SECRET Nøgne mixes
British Marris Otter malt with American
C-hops, including Cascade, Centenneal,
Chinook, and Columbus.

Saison

SAISON **6.5**% ABV

East Kent Goldings and Crystal hops
and Belgian ale yeast produce a light
and refreshing brew, available all year
but ideal in summer.

Imperial Stout

IMPERIAL STOUT **9**% ABV

A dark, rich ale with a generous
sweetness and bitterness coming
from the roasted malts.

Ochakovo

44, Riabinivaya, Moscow, **RUSSIA**
www.ochakovo.ru

Ochakovo is the last independent Russian brewery, and is trying to remain so. Its original brewhouse has been transformed into a museum, which takes visitors, step-by-step, through the brewing process and features many exhibits from the 19th century.

BREWING SECRET In 2005, Ochakovo launched an unpasteurized, unfiltered "live" beer, aimed at the health market.

Ochakovo Classic

LAGER 5% ABV
Corn-yellow in color, with intense malt overtones and a hoppy finish.

Ochakovo Ruby

VIENNA LAGER 3.9% ABV
Pale ruby in color, with aromas of winter fruits and floral notes, it has strong hints of caramel on the palate.

Okell's

Douglas, Isle of Man,
IM2 1QG **ENGLAND**
www.okells.co.uk

Dr. William Okell's steam-
powered brewery—which he
designed himself in 1874—was
regarded as one of the most
sophisticated in the world at the
time. Okell's new plant, which it
moved to in 1994, is the modern
equivalent. It is controlled by
computers rather than steam,
but the passion and commitment
to quality beer production
remains unaltered.

Doctor Okell's IPA

INDIA PALE ALE **4.4**% ABV
Potential sweetness, offset by a
high hopping regime for overall
roundness, spiced by lemon notes.

Okell's Bitter

BITTER **3.7**% ABV
Light colored and complexly flavored,
with hints of honey and a long-lingering
dry finish.

Ommegang

656 County Highway 33
Cooperstown, NY 13326, **USA**
www.ommegang.com

Owned by Belgium's Duvel
Moortgat, Brewery Ommegang
has brewed ales in the Belgian
tradition since 1997, selling
limited quantities across much
of the US. It hosts one of the
nation's most outstanding beer
festivals, Belgium Comes to
Coopers-town, each summer in
the picturesque brewery grounds
outside of town.

Hennepin
SAISON 7.7% ABV
Spicy and peppery throughout. Yeasty
notes, citrus more apparent on the palate.
Tart and dry.

Ommegang Abbey Ale
BELGIAN STRONG DARK ALE 8.5% ABV
The flagship ale, produced in the
spirit of a Christmas beer. Rich and
chocolatey, with underlying liquorice
and festive spices.

Orkney

Stromness, Orkney,
KW16 3LT **SCOTLAND**
www.orkneybrewery.co.uk

Commendable ecological
awareness allows the brewery's
waste water to be filtered through
two neighboring lochs that
support fish and waterfowl. It
was first set up in 1988, and then
thoroughly modernized in 1994.
In 2008, the brewery expanded,
adding a visitor center and shop.
Its output was also increased.

Dark Island

STRONG BITTER **4.6**% ABV
Ruby-red and mysterious, with
blackcurrant fruit on the nose and
a full-roasted malt palate.

Skullsplitter

BARLEY WINE **8.5**% ABV
Forcefully malty nose; hints of
apple, spicy hop, and some nut
in the complex flavorings.

Panil (Torrechiara)

Strada Pilastro 35/a,
43010 Torrechiara (PR), **ITALY**
www.panilbeer.com

Renzo Losi, a biology graduate, got his brewing break in 2000, when his winemaker father gave him permission to make beer at the family's vineyard estate, south of Parma.

BREWING SECRET The links with the family winemaking tradition are retained in the use of oak barrels and spumante yeasts.

Panil Barriquée Sour
FLEMISH SOUR RED 8% ABV
The flagship ale, barrel-aged for three months. Sour, vinous, and uncompromising.

Divina
WILD BEER 5.5% ABV
Spontaneously fermented by being left, uncovered, on the back of a truck in a field overnight. Sweet-sour, yeasty, and citrussy.

Piccolo Birrificio

Via iv Novembre 20,
18035 Apricale (IM), **ITALY**
www.piccolobirrificio.com

This microbrewery, founded in
2005, is housed in a former
olive-oil mill in the lovely
medieval village of Apricale,
near the French border. Brewer
Lorenzo Bottoni produces a
range of fine ales under the
brand name of Nüa ("naked"),
including some amazing
brews using unusual local
fruits and plants.

Sesonette

BELGIAN SAISON 6.5% ABV
Matured in Chardonnay barrels with
spices and local chinotto peel (from a
small, bitter citrus fruit).

Chiostro

SPICED ALE 5% ABV
Spiced with *Artemisia absinthium*
(wormwood), then fermented with
Trappist yeasts, giving complex and
unique aromas and flavors.

Pietra

Route de la Marana,
20600 Furiani, **FRANCE**
www.brasseriepietra.com

The first Corsican brewery
in history opened in 1996.
Brewers Armelle and Dominique
Sialelli use raw materials native
to the island, such as *maquis*
herbs and chestnut flour, which
forms an ingredient rather than
just a flavoring in their Pietra
beer. *Biera Corsa* has been a
great success, both in Corsica
and overseas.

Colomba
WHEAT BEER 5% ABV
Very fresh and sharp, with unusual
aromas of arbutus, myrtle, and juniper.
A refreshing summer beer.

Pietra
AMBER LAGER 6% ABV
Elegant flavors of toasted malts,
nuttiness, and a slight bitterness.

Pilsner Urquell

U Prazdroje 7, 304 97 Plzeň,
CZECH REPUBLIC
www.pilsner-urquell.cz

The Czechs have blessed us
with the microwave oven, soft
contact lenses, and beer that
changed the world. It was,
however, a Bavarian who was
the key player in the Pilsner
Urquell story. As a young brewer,
Josef Groll presented the nation
with its first pilsner on October 4,
1842. This sensational clear
golden beer spread across
Europe like wildfire from its
"original source."

Pilsner Urquell

CLASSIC PILSNER **4.4**% ABV
The ideal one-and-a-half inch (35 mm)
tight head leaves a lacing down the
glass with every sip of spiced leaf and
preserved fruit flavors, developing
a sweet malt piquancy and long,
enveloping finish.

PRAGUE, CZECH REPUBLIC

The city of Prague is one of the world's greatest beer destinations. And where better to start a beer trail than in the Old Town Square (Staroměstské náměstí), location of the famous 15th-century Astronomical Clock—one of the world's oldest clocks still in working order. Many bars edge the square, each spilling out on to the cobbles with seating and canopies.

2 U ZLATÉHO TYGRA
One of the Old Town's most atmospheric and oldest bars, U Zlatého Tygra is crowded with small tables, which always seem to be full with locals deep in energetic conversations—so be prepared to stand. It's a favorite of the writer and former Czech President Václav Havel, and President Clinton has also drunk here. The unfiltered Pilsner Urquell is said to be the best in Prague. *Husova 17, Prague*

3 U PINKASŮ
In 1843 U Pinkasů was the first bar in Prague to serve Pilsner Urquell, and it is still available today. The bar was saved from extinction in 2000, when it was extensively refurbished. A more recent refurbishment has opened up more of the building. *Jungmannovo nám, 16/15, Prague*

1 OLD TOWN SQUARE
Here it is possible to sit outside and savor a beer, while watching the thousands of visitors who now flock to the Czech capital. Displays of folk dancing and music can often be enjoyed here too.

4 NOVOMĚSTSKÝ PIVOVAR

An Art Deco-style entrance leads visitors down an alleyway of shops to this wood-paneled brewery, pub, and restaurant. Unfiltered light and dark beers are available. The food is unashamedly Czech, with specialties such a goulash, tripe soup, and roast knuckle of pork. *Vodickova 20, Prague*

5 PIVODUM

The Pivodum restaurant and bar is dominated by gleaming coppers. Traditional Czech beers are served, as well as other interesting brews, including a sour cherry beer, a coffee beer, and Samp—a beer champagne. Groups can order eight beers for the price of seven, and they are served in a large giraffelike container. A sample tray of eight beers is available too. *Ječná/Lípová 15, Prague*

6 U FLEKŮ

Crowded it may be, a haunt of many tourists it certainly is, but U Fleků should not be missed. Brewing began here in 1499, and it is said to be the world's oldest brewpub. It comprises many large rooms, including one for a booming oompah band. It has a small museum and daily brewery tours. The superb house beer is Flekovsky tmavy lezáck, which comes in dark and light versions. *Kremencova 11, Prague*

TRAIL OR TOUR STATS
1 hour, plus drinking time
3 miles (5 km)

0m   200 yards
0m   200m

De Prael

Helicopterstraat 13-15, 1059 CE
Amsterdam, **NETHERLANDS**
www.deprael.nl

Set up with the help of
government grants, Amsterdam's
smallest brewery has a workforce
made up of recovering
psychiatric patients. The first
choice of name—De Parel ("The
Pearl")—had to be changed when
Budels complained that it
infringed on the copyright
of their Parel beer. The solution
was simply to shuffle the letters
of the name around.

Heintje
WITBIER 5.4% ABV
Unspiced, but with prominent citrus
aromas, a touch of fruit, and an
unexpectedly hoppy finish.

Mary
BARLEY WINE 9.6% ABV
Neither malt nor hops dominate this
fruity strong ale, laced with pepper,
toffee, and caramel.

Quilmes

Tte. Gral. Juan D. Peron 667 103,
Buenos Aires, **ARGENTINA**
www.quilmes.com.ar

The dominant beer in Argentina, Quilmes is now part of the InBev embrace. Like many breweries in South America, it was begun by a German, the brewery and malt plant being founded in the 1880s by Otto Bemberg. "Quilmes" derives from an indigenous name for the place where the brewery is located.

Quilmes Cristal
LAGER **4.9**% ABV

Thin and pale, with no aromatic distractions. Surprisingly drinkable, though, with refreshing sweetness.

Quilmes Stout
STOUT **4.8**% ABV

Three malts clamor for attention—but the expected coffee flavors are overwhelmed by sweetness.

Radegast

739 51 Nošovice, **CZECH REPUBLIC**
www.radegast.cz

Radegast, roughly meaning "dear guest," was the Slavic god of fertility and crops, and consequently became proclaimed god of hospitality too. Despite its nominal connections with the dawn of time, the brewery actually began operating only in 1970. It continues to be one of the country's most technologically advanced and best equipped beer producers.

Radegast Original
PILSNER 4% ABV
A light malt and spiced hop nose, malt-sweet flavors and a crisp, grainy bitterness.

Radegast Premium
PREMIUM LAGER 5% ABV
A characteristic herbal hoppy aroma and medium-sweet malt intensity dwell on cereal notes.

Refsvindinge Brewery

Nyborgvej 80,
DK-5853 Ørbæk, **DENMARK**
www.bryggerietrefsvindinge.dk

Since 1885, four generations
have run this farmhouse
brewery. It was among the first
to brew ales in Denmark and is
credited with developing Danish
white beer (*hvidtøl*) and the
old-style smoked "ship's beer"
(*skibsøl*), as well as two varieties
of beer for children (not entirely
alcohol free!).

Ale No.16
BROWN ALE 5.7% ABV
Well rounded, typical dark ale using
original English yeast to produce a sweet,
fresh taste.

Mors Stout
PORTER 5.7% ABV
Dark, smooth porter brewed using malt
that has been roasted with cocoa beans.

Ridna Marka

71 Mikgorod str.Radomyshl,
UKRAINE
www.etalon-beer.com.ua/en

Beermaking in Radomyshl dates from 1886, when this brewery was founded by the Czech Albrechtam brothers. They found that the soft water here was ideal for brewing. The modern brewery has adapted Bavarian technology to Ukrainian ingredients.

BREWING SECRET The brewhouse has been specifically designed to produce unfiltered, genuine wheat beers.

Etalon Weissbier
WHEAT BEER 5% ABV
Spicy with a rich, creamy malt note and a long, quenching flavor and finish. Hints of bananas and vanilla.

Rouget de Lisle

Rue des Vernes,
39140 Bletterans, **FRANCE**
www.larougetdelisle.com

Opened in 2002, and named after
the locally born composer of
The Marseillaise, this brewery
develops up to 15 new beers each
year, some of them using local
ingredients instead of hops for
their bitter notes.

BREWING SECRET Among the
ingredients used to replace hops are
wormwood, dandelion, blackcurrant,
and gentian.

Fourche Du Diable

LAGER **5.4**% ABV
Amber in color; aromas of spring flowers
and an unusual bitter note contributed
by gentian roots.

Abisinthe

LAGER **6**% ABV
Golden and very refreshing, with aromas
of mint, balm, and the special bitterness
of wormwood.

Saint Arnold

2522 Fairway Park Drive
Houston, TX 77092, **USA**
www.saintarnold.com

The oldest surviving and largest
craft brewery in Texas was
founded in 1994. Saint Arnold
grew out of its "micro" status in
2007, although it continues to
sell its beer only within the state
borders. Austrian-born St. Arnold
is one of the patron saints of
beer; the brewery's fermenters
are named after other saints.

Amber
AMBER ALE 5.5% ABV
Caramel and fermentation fruit, with
bright, spicy hops providing balance.
Excellent on cask.

Elissa IPA
INDIA PALE ALE 6.6% ABV
Delightfully hoppy throughout,
brimming with grapefruit character.
Big and juicy, with rich malt to match
the decided bitterness.

Samuel Adams

30 Germania Street, Boston,
MA 02130 **USA**
www.samueladams.com

The name Samuel Adams has been
synonymous with craft beer since
Boston Beer Company was one
of just a few specialty beer sellers
in the country. The company
launched the brand in 1984,
when it contracted production to
mainstream producers with excess
capacity. Boston Beer has since
purchased some of those
breweries and produces much of
its own beer. The company holds
an employees' homebrew contest
each year, with the winner's beer
being sold commercially.

Boston Lager
VIENNA LAGER 4.9% ABV
Complex flowery/piney nose. Full-bodied,
with caramel in the middle, and a
satisfyingly dry finish.

Utopias
STRONG ALE 27% ABV
The strongest beer in the world, aged in
brandy and port barrels. Serve and sip
like a rare cognac.

BAMBERG, GERMANY

Can there be a better place in the world to drink beer? This beautiful, baroque island city, on the banks of the Regnitz River and the Main-Donau Canal, is in the Upper Franconia region of Bavaria. It is built on medieval foundations and is home to 70,000 people and 11 breweries. The city is a base for many US army personnel and their families—and they have helped, no doubt, to take the fame of this beer paradise around the world.

3 THE BRAUEREI SPEZIAL'S

The Brauerei Spezial's is very much a locals' bar, decorated with laughter and conversations. Its Specizil Rauchbier has subtle, soft toffee flavors and even a hint of burnt straw. Spezial uses smoked malt in at least four of its other beers. By the bar is a serving hatch, where locals come to fill containers with beer for drinking at home. *Obere Königstrasse 10, Bamberg (www.brauerei-spezial.de)*

1 KLOSTERBRAU

Beer has been brewed at Klosterbrau since 1533. Down a cobbled street, time seems to slip away in this fairytale of a brewery tap. The range includes a schwarzbier, braunbier, weizen, pils, and a bock. *Oberre Muhlbruck 3, Bamberg (www.klosterbraueu.de)*

2 OLD TOWN HALL

The river is never far away in Bamberg. The stroll to Brauerei Spezial's passes the spectacular medieval stone-and-timbered Old Town Hall, which seems precariously balanced on the footings of an ancient bridge. Take a moment to admire it before heading on to the Brauerei Spezial's.

4 BRAUEREI FÄSSLA

Directly opposite Brauerei Spezial's is Brauerei Fässla. Brewing started here in 1649. The brewery tap has a comfortable, wood-paneled, country-style room, and above it is a small hotel. The brewery's logo—a dwarf rolling a barrel of beer—decorates the glasses and dark furniture. Fässla's easy-drinking Lagerbier melds malty flavors with a fresh, soft bitterness. *Obere Königsstrasse 19–21, Bamberg (www.faessla.de)*

5 SCHLENKERLA

Vibrant and friendly, Schlenkerla is Bamberg's best-known bar and restaurant. The warmth of its world-famous rauchbier, with its smoked whiskey and cheese overtones, is as warm as the welcome. Tables are often shared, and the atmosphere is highly convivial. Beer is the social lubricant and the perfect accompaniment to robust Bavarian dishes such as onions stuffed with beery meatballs. *Dominikanerstrasse 6, Bamberg (www.smokebeer.com)*

6 AMBRÄUSIANUM

Opposite Schlenkerla is the Ambräusianum. Here, the brewing vessels can be seen, which makes it seem more like a modern brewpub than one of Bamberg's traditional establishments, and it is a relative newcomer, being open only since 2004. Weekend breakfasts comprise a glass of wheat beer with three locally made Bavarian veal sausages and a pretzel. *Dominikanerstrasse 10, Bamberg (www.ambraeusianum.de)*

7 WEINSTUBE PIZZINI

The exterior of the Weinstube Pizzini is somewhat unprepossessing, and do not be deterred by its name—it is neither a wine bar nor a pizza restaurant. Inside this small, brown decorated and time-worn bar, there is a warm-hearted welcome and the opportunity to try Fässla and Spezial beers, as well as a dunkel from Andechser. *Ober Sandstrasse 17, Bamberg*

TRAIL OR TOUR STATS
30 mins, plus drinking time
2 miles (3 km)

Sharp's

Wadebridge, Cornwall,
PL27 6NU **ENGLAND**
www.sharpsbrewery.co.uk

Facing the Atlantic from the
Cornish coast undoubtedly has
an influence, not only on how the
beer is made, but also on people's
objectives and horizons. Sharp's
commendable approach to
sustainable energy and water
recycling is echoed by an
energetic attitude, which is
inspiring for the future of
cask ale production.

Doom Bar
BITTER 4% ABV
Spicy resinous hop aromas and sweet,
delicate malts blend with dried fruit
and assertive bitterness.

Atlantic IPA
INDIA PALE ALE 4.8% ABV
Four hop varieties are added at different
stages to create cotton candy aromas and
delicate flavors.

Shepherd Neame

Faversham, Kent,
ME13 7AX **ENGLAND**
www.shepherdneame.co.uk

It didn't take 12th-century monks long to discover that Faversham's pure spring water could be combined with locally grown malting barley to produce particularly fine ale. When the town's mayor founded a brewery in 1698 he launched the country's longest-surviving brewery, which was by 1864 called Shepherd Neame still run by the Neame family.

BREWING SECRET The brewery still makes use of mash tuns made from Russian teak, installed in 1914.

Bishop's Finger
STRONG BITTER 5% ABV
Generously fruity, with banana and pear prominent, a biscuit-rich maltiness, and dried fruit flavors.

Spitfire
PREMIUM BITTER 4.5% ABV
A underlying deep maltiness is combined with a subtle hint of toffee and boldly fruity citrus hops.

Shongweni / Robson's

B1 Shongweni Valley, Shongweni,
near Durban, KwaZulu-Natal,
SOUTH AFRICA
www.shongwenibrewery.com

Shongweni mainly produces
bottle-conditioned beers, using
the infusion mash technique and
fermentation in open-top vessels.
All its beers are unfiltered and
unpasteurized. The family-owned
brewery stands out in a local
market dominated by mass-
produced lagers. It exports to
the UK and elsewhere.

Robson's Durban Pale Ale
INDIA PALE ALE 5.7% ABV
Brewed with Pale malt, and Cascade and
Challenger hops. Crisp, fruity, and
well-balanced.

Robson's East Coast Ale
GOLDEN ALE 4% ABV
A smooth and refreshing golden
ale, made with a single malt variety along
with Brewers Gold and Challenger hops.

Siebensternbräu

Siebensterngasse 19,
A-1070 Vienna, **AUSTRIA**
www.7stern.at

Siebensternbräu was the first
brewpub in Austria to brew
specialty beers—IPA, chili,
and fruit flavored. Owner Sigi
Flitter also helped reintroduce
many of Austria's indigenous but
forgotten beer styles.

BREWING SECRET The range varies
with each season, but expect a wheat beer
in summer and a smoked in winter.

Rauchbock
SMOKED BOCK 7.9% ABV
Intense smoky nose; full, almost sweet
body, with hints of chocolate and
liquorice, and a smoky finish.

Prager Dunkles
DARK LAGER 4.5% ABV
While most dark beers in Austria are
terribly sweet, this one is dry. Intense
toasty notes, very little hop aroma.
Roasty finish.

Sierra Nevada

1075 East 20th Street, Chico,
CA 95928, **USA**
www.sierranevada.com

Sierra Nevada Brewing has been
introducing beer drinkers to
citrussy, piney Northwest hops
since 1981 and the brewery
continues to act as a matchmaker
between beer drinkers and hops.
Sierra Nevada is also an industry
leader in good environmental
practice. It has commissioned the
first phase of one of the country's
largest private solar installations,
which will bring it close to its
goal of generating 100 percent
of its energy needs.

Pale Ale
PALE ALE 5.6% ABV
Piney, grapefruity Cascade hops play
against malt fruitiness on both the nose
and the palate.

Bigfoot
BARLEY WINE 9.6% ABV
Earthy and chewy, with prominent citric
hops and whiskeylike rich malts. Boldly
bitter when young.

Silly / Mynsbrug Hen

2, Ville Basse, B7830 Silly, **BELGIUM**
www.silly-beer.com

Established in the 19th century, this family brewery walks a fine line between maintaining traditions and employing technical developments geared toward satisfying changing market niches. A *saison* is still produced—bottled and, better yet, on draft—and they have recently launched a beer flavored with rum and named after a regional rock band.

Silly Saison
SAISON 5.2% ABV
Fruity, madeiralike, thin-bodied. Even when young, this is more like an oud bruin than a real *saison*.

Scotch Silly
SCOTCH ALE 8% ABV
Scotch ales are a Walloon tradition. This very malty dark beer is full-bodied and rich.

Simonds Farsons Cisk

The Brewery, Notabile Road, Mriehel, BKR 01, **MALTA**
www.farsons.com

Wherever the British army went, beer was soon to follow, and this brewery was built in lavish Art Deco style at the end of World War II in 1946. The site is being redeveloped, with the old brewing vessels at the heart of a visitor center.

BREWING SECRET It brews the potent XS (9% ABV) for the export market.

Farsons Lacto
MILK STOUT 3.8% ABV
Soft on the tongue, this black beer is a classic milk stout, with lactose added after fermentation.

Hopleaf Extra
ALE 5% ABV
English malt, along with Challenger and Target hops, produce a complex beer with a refreshing bitter finish.

Sinebrychoff

Oy Sinebrychoff Ab,
Sinebrychoffinaukio 1 PL 87,
FL-04201 Kerava, **FINLAND**
www.koff.fi

Sinebrychoff is part of the
Carlsberg Group, and its
abbreviated name and main
brand range, Koff, is one of the
most popular in Finland. It is the
oldest Nordic brewery, founded
by Russian Nikolai Sinebrychoff
in 1819.

BREWING SECRET Karhupanimo, their
new microbrewery, is producing a range
of hand-crafted lagers.

Sinebrychoff Porter
IMPERIAL STOUT 7.2% ABV
Robust and brimming with coffee flavors,
this beer has a long, warming finish.

Karhu III
LAGER 4.6% ABV
Described by the brewer as "untamed."
Full-bodied, with stronger flavors of hops
and malt than are usual for a lager.

Smuttynose

225 Heritage Avenue
Portsmouth, NH 03801, **USA**
www.smuttynose.com

Although Smuttynose Brewing
has earned a reputation for its
carefully balanced offerings, the
brewery was also one of the first
to embrace "extreme beers,"
launching a Big Beer Series in
1998. Succeeding on all fronts, it
found itself out of room by 2007,
and plans to relocate its brewing,
still close to Portsmouth.

Shoals Pale Ale

PALE ALE 5% ABV
First made at the Portsmouth pub.
Pleasant fruity/biscuit palate gives
way to a crisp American hop finish.

Robust Porter

PORTER 5.7% ABV
Rich dark fruits and chocolate, well
blended throughout. Rich, roasty flavors
leave a strong impression for a medium-
strength beer.

Snake River

265 S. Millward Street
Jackson, WY 83001, **USA**
www.snakeriverbrewing.com

Located in central Jackson, with
a view of Snow King Mountain
and standing but a few miles
from the Jackson Hole ski resort,
Snake River brewpub occupies an
old cinder-block warehouse. It
has twice won Small Brewery of
the Year at the Great American
Beer Festival.

Zonker Stout
STOUT **5.8%** ABV
Roasted barley sets a bold tone, with
chocolate (almost sweet) underneath.
Pleasingly dry finish.

Lager
VIENNA LAGER **6%** ABV
Golden, with a thick white head.
Malt-accented, clean toasted and
caramel flavors, drying hop finish.

Staropramen

Nádražni 84, 150 54 Prague 5,
CZECH REPUBLIC
www.staropramen.com

Far-sighted developers situated the Smíchov Brewery in Prague's future industrial area, where demand for beer was assured. From the start, Staropramen—Prague's biggest brewer—was perceived as a Czech beer for Czech people, which gave it an advantage among nationalist-leaning consumers. Today it is owned by global giant InBev.

Staropramen Dark Beer
DARK BEER 4.5% ABV
Its light body loops around malty caramel, liquorice, and aniseed notes to a floral finale.

Staropramen Premium Lager
PREMIUM LAGER 5% ABV
A rich floral bite unveils a full-bodied satisfier with a riz ("just right") finish.

St. Austell

St. Austell, Cornwall,
PL25 4BY **ENGLAND**
www.staustellbrewery.co.uk

The enterprising spirit that
drove Walter Hicks to mortgage
his farm for £1,500 in 1851 and
set up a brewery remains at the
core of today's business. Many
of his descendants are still
involved in the company—in
its estate of 168 pubs and in
the brewery, which produces
in excess of 40,000 barrels
(6.5 million liters) annually.

Tribute

BITTER 4.2% ABV
Specially grown Cornish Gold barley
delivers a rich biscuit aroma, tempered
by intense fruit flavors.

St. Austell IPA

INDIA PALE ALE 3.4% ABV
Full of flavor and packed with fresh
hoppiness; the rounded palate arrives
with veils of caramel.

St Christoffel

Metaalweg 10, 6045 JB Roermond,
NETHERLANDS
www.christoffelbier.nl

Operating since 1986, St
Christoffel is one of the oldest
Dutch micros, founded (but no
longer run) by Leo Brand, a
member of the Brand brewing
dynasty. It produces the very
best lagers brewed in
the Netherlands.

BREWING SECRET The Robertus beer is
a rare example of a Münchner dark lager
that's true to the Bavarian style.

Christoffel Blond
PILS 6% ABV
Spicy hop flavors burst from the glass
—basil, mint, ginger, grapefruit, and
cloves are all there.

Christoffel Robertus
MÜNCHNER 6% ABV
The nutty flavor of Munich malt runs
right through this beer, flanked by
biscuit, toast, and toffee.

Stiegl

Kendlerstrasse 1,
A-5017 Salzburg, **AUSTRIA**
www.stiegl.at

Austria's largest independent
brewery produces Austria's
single most successful beer,
Goldbräu. The brewery itself
dates back to 1492 and, over
time, has built up a splendid
collection of beer-related exhibits
for the "Brauwelt"—the largest
museum on the continent
entirely devoted to brewing.

Goldbräu
AUSTRIAN MÄRZEN-TYPE
LAGER **4.9%** ABV
Relatively low bitterness and a hint
of malty sweetness in the aroma and
on the palate.

Paracelsus Zwickl
ORGANIC LAGER **5%** ABV
Unfiltered, so hazy orange in hue; aromas
of malt and yeast; medium body and very
low bitterness.

Brauhaus Sternen

Hohenzornstrasse 2, CH-8500
Frauenfeld, **SWITZERLAND**
www.brauhaussternen.ch

This is an intriguing brewpub,
set up on the site of the
Aktienbrauerei Frauenfeld,
where Martin Wartmann created
Ittinger (now brewed at Calanda).
The present brewery was built in
2003 with financial help from
many prominent European
brewers eager to see Martin brew
interesting beers, some in limited
editions ("Nur für Freunde"—
"for friends only").

Wartmann's Nur Für Freunde No1

BELGIAN DUBBEL **9.6**% ABV

Chocolaty, slightly sweet aroma. Full-
bodied and fruity (ripe plums); very mild
bitterness in the finish.

Honey Brown Ale

BROWN ALE **6**% ABV

Sweet and fruity. Quite refreshing for its
strength. Very low bitterness and a hint
of honey in the finish.

Sul Brasileira

BR 392, Km 05, Santa Maria—
RS, 97000, **BRAZIL**
http://xingubeer.com

Local folklore says that Sul
Brasileira's Xingu beer is the
daughter of a beer brewed in
ancient times by pioneering
Amazonian brewsters. The name
Xinghu (pronounced "shin-goo")
is a tributary of the Amazon
River, which is home to the few
surviving cultures and species
of native Amazonian life.

Xingu Black Beer
SCHWARZBIER 4.7% ABV
Dark in color, but light and sweet
to taste. Still in the glass, its head
soon disappears.

Švyturys-Utenos

Kuliu Vartu g. 7, Klaipeda,
LITHUANIA
www.svyturys.lt/en

Brewing began here in 1784, making this the oldest brewery in Lithuania. The company has a reputation for the quality of its beers and has won several international brewing awards. It is open to the public for tours twice a week for groups of five to 25 (via the tourist office at www. klaipedainfo.lt).

BREWING SECRET All the employees give their feedback on each new brew.

Švyturys Ekstra
DORTMUND LAGER 5.2% ABV
Clear and golden, it has a firm white head, an intense aroma of hops, and a slight bitterness.

Švyturio
LAGER 5% ABV
Translucent gold in color, it has a good balance of rich malt and bitter hops. In Lithuania it's known simply as "red," due to its label color.

Teerenpeli

Hämeenkatu 19, Lahti, **FINLAND**
www.teerenpeli.com

Teerenpeli operates breweries,
bars, and restaurants in
Helsinki, Lahti, and Tampere.
Its first brewery was founded
in 1995. A new brewery and
whiskey distillery opened in
2002, set within the Restaurant
Taivaanranta in Lahti.
Teerenpeli's beers have
won medals at the Helsinki
Beer Festival.

Laiskajaakko
DARK LAGER 4.5% ABV
Full-bodied, malty dark lager, brewed
with Crystal 50 and Black malt, and
Hallertau hops.

Onnenpekka
PALE LAGER 4.7% ABV
Golden and refreshing. Made with Pilsner
barley malt from the Lahti region, and
pure water from the Salpausselkä area.

Terrapin

255 Newton Bridge Road
Athens, GA 30607, **USA**
www.terrapinbeer.com

Spike Buckowski and John Cochran began shipping beer from their own brewhouse early in 2008, almost six years after the Terrapin Beer Company started selling contract-brewed Rye Pale Ale. That beer was an immediate hit, as was the Monster Beer Tour, a series of strong beers released after Georgia raised its 6 percent ABV cap on beer.

Rye Pale Ale

PALE ALE 5.3% ABV

Rye blends with bright grapefruit, adds texture to fruit fermentation, and complements late bitterness.

Wake-n-Bake Coffee Oatmeal Imperial Stout

IMPERIAL STOUT 8.1% ABV

It's all in the name, along with chocolate-covered dark fruits.

Theakston

Masham, North Yorkshire,
HG4 4YD **ENGLAND**
www.theakstons.co.uk

Ownership battles may have
swept in numerous changes
during its 180-year history but,
fortunately today, tradition
survives and thrives. Now
returned to the Theakston
family following Scottish &
Newcastle's management, the
company lives up to the name
of its most famous beer—
Peculier, a 12th-century word
meaning "particular."

Old Peculier
STRONG BITTER **5.6**% ABV
Rich and deep dark ruby in hue, with
a mellow fruit aroma and a malty,
full-bodied flavor.

Black Bull Bitter
BITTER **3.9**% ABV
Bright amber colored, with a crisp,
dry palate weaving through citrus
fruit flavors.

Three Boys Brewery

Unit 10, Garlands Rd, Woolston,
Christchurch, **NEW ZEALAND**
www.threeboysbrewery.co.nz

Microbiologist Ralph Bungard
employs a broad range of
yeasts to produce tasty Kiwi
interpretations of classic beer
styles. The senior "Boy"—the
others are his sons Marek
and Quinn.

BREWING SECRET The brewery's
limited release seasonal brews include
an excellent Oyster Stout in winter and
a fragrant Golden Ale in summer.

Three Boys Wheat
WITBIER 5% ABV
Plenty of zesty lemon and coriander
notes, with a hint of ginger.
A spritzy and quenching brew.

Three Boys Porter
ROBUST PORTER 5.2% ABV
Rich mocha notes dominate a silky
palate, while heavily roasted grain
and hops compete in the dry finish.

Three Floyds

9750 Indiana Parkway
Munster, IN 46321, **USA**
www.threefloyds.com

Beginning with its flagship
Alpha King in 1996, Three
Floyds Brewing had lived by
the philosophy of brewmaster
Nick Floyd: "I love the smell of
hops in the morning. It smells
like victory."

BREWING SECRET The annual release
of Dark Lord Russian Imperial Stout sells
out in one day, with customers driving
hundreds of miles to buy it.

Alpha King
PALE ALE 6% ABV
Opens with a rush of citrus fruits. Firm
malt backbone, matched by hop oils.
Prolonged bitterness.

Gumballhead
US WHEAT BEER 4.8% ABV
Citrus and orchard fruits on the
nose, followed by wheat tartness
and hops throughout.

Titanic

Burslem, Staffordshire,
ST6 1JL **ENGLAND**
www.titanicbrewery.co.uk

What began with brewing for demonstration purposes on log-fired Victorian equipment developed into the production of in excess of 17 million pints a year. Ecologically friendly business practices—recycling and conservation—are a priority. The name is taken from the world's most famous passenger ship, whose captain, John Edward Smith, was born nearby.

Titanic Stout

STOUT **4.5**% ABV

Full roast, preserved fruit aromas; the malt-influenced palate accentuates more fruit and liquorice tiers.

Best Bitter

BEST BITTER **3.5**% ABV

Straw colored, with a waft of sulfur in the aroma and persistent hop flavorings.

Topvar

Krusovska cesta 2092,
Topolcany, **SLOVAKIA**
www.topvar.sk

The brewery operates at two sites
in Slovakia: Topolcany and Velký
Šariš. In 2000, the brewery
launched a beer called Brigita,
named after the Slovak finance
minister Brigita Schmögnerovà.
A popular beer, it remained on
sale for some time after her
resignation in 2002. The company
is now owned by SABMiller.

Topvar Svetlé

LAGER **5.2**% ABV

A sunburst of yellow tones, with a thin
white head. This beer has an attractive
nose, with plenty of citrus fruit flavors.

T

Traquair

Innerleithen, Peeblesshire,
EH44 6PW **SCOTLAND**
www.traquair.co.uk

The 18th-century brewing
equipment in a house where
Bonnie Prince Charlie once
sought refuge remained
untouched until their rediscovery
in 1965. Since then, they have
been put to use for brewing in
authentic style.

BREWING SECRET Unusually in this
day and age, Traquair's beers are
fermented in oak over a seven-day period.

Traquair House Ale
BARLEY WINE 7.2% ABV
A dark and oaky winter brew, with
ripe malt, fruit cake, and sweet
sherry mystique.

Jacobite Ale
BARLEY WINE 8% ABV
Herbal notes from the use of coriander
warm the bittersweet chocolate and
port wine flavors.

La Trappe

Eindhovenseweg 3, Berkel-Enschot,
NETHERLANDS
www.latrappe.nl

There are just seven genuine
Trappist breweries in the world;
Koningshoeven (better known as
La Trappe) is the only one outside
Belgium. The monastery had
problems recruiting new monks,
and that was one of the factors
that prompted the sale of the
brewery to Bavaria. Brewing still
takes place within the monastery
grounds under the supervision
of the monks.

La Trappe Witte Trappist
WITBIER 5.5% ABV

Unspiced, but a subtle use of aromatic
hops more than compensates, providing
delicious citrus and pepper flavors.

La Trappe Tripel
STRONG ALE 8% ABV

Sweetness and fruit give way to coriander,
orange, and hop bitterness in this
supremely balanced beer.

Tsingtao

Hong Kong Road, Central,
Qinqdao, 266071 **CHINA**
www.tsingtaobeer.com

The Tsingtao Brewery was
founded in 1903 by German
settlers in Qingdao. Today it is
part owned by American giants
Anheuser-Busch, which is
currently undertaking a massive
investment in new breweries on
the China mainland. The
company runs over 40 breweries
and malt plants in 18 provinces
across China.

Tsingtao
LAGER 4.8% ABV

Crisp, slightly malty flavor and nutty
sweet taste. The color is a bright
yellow; aroma grainy, with a hint of
sweetness. A high level of carbonation
makes it very fizzy.

U Medvídků

Na Perštýně 7, 100 01 Prague 1,
CZECH REPUBLIC
www.umedvidku.cz

The restaurant and brewhouse
date back to 1466, though the
brewery has been reinstalled in
recent years—along with
extensions and additions to the
pension, which retains its
original Gothic rafters and
Renaissance painted ceilings.
This is one of the biggest beer
halls in Prague, and it hosted
the city's first cabaret.

Oldgott Barique Ležák
PILSNER 5.2% ABV
Earthy and melon-fruity aromas, yeasty
characteristics developing into a roasted
malt, caramel infusion.

X-Beer
SPECIALTY BEER 12.6% ABV (VARIABLE)
Matured for 28 weeks in oak vessels
for an elaborate, sweet flavor and
indulgent complexity.

Union

Pivovarniška ulica 2,
1000 Ljubljana, **SLOVENIA**
www.pivo-union.si

This brewery was founded in 1864 by the Kozler family, but state-of-the-art technology makes it one of the most modern in Slovenia. A fascinating museum takes visitors through the brewing process. However, you have to be there on the first Tuesday morning of the month to enjoy it.

Union Lager
LAGER 5% ABV
A Slovenian favorite. A sweet, golden beer, it has corn overtones.

ČRNI Baron / Black Baron
STOUT 5.2% ABV
A dark dessert beer, rich with caramel notes and aromas; its finish is warming but could be longer.

United Breweries

Bengaluru, **INDIA**
www.theubgroup.com

It is said the company's logo—
a Pegasus—once carried a cask
of beer between its wings as a gift
to the gods. Its Kingfisher brand
is the flying leader in India's
soaring beer market, and what
once was a company that
supplied beer to the troops of the
British Empire has now acquired
a worldwide reputation.

Kingfisher

LAGER 5% ABV

Brewed under license in many
countries. It has a crisp taste with
a sweetish overtone.

London Pilsner 5.0

LAGER 5% ABV

Thin yellow color, some hop aroma, and
a sweetish after taste, it smells of grass.

Upstream

514 South 11th Street
Omaha, NE 68102, **USA**
www.upstreambrewing.com

Since opening in 1996 as part of
an "unlinked chain" started by
Wynkoop Brewery, Upstream
(a translation of the Native
American name for Omaha)
has gained independence,
opened a second pub, and
brewed varieties of beers not
previously found in Nebraska.

BREWING SECRET Developments
include barrel-ageing, and the use
of wild yeast.

Batch 1000 Barley Wine
BARLEY WINE 10.2% ABV
Caramel and vinous on the nose and
palate, blending with lively fruity esters.
Rich, almost chewy, palate.

Grand Cru
BELGIAN STRONG ALE 9% ABV
Aged for a year in oak wine barrels.
Earthy and woody nose, delicate
citrus and honey on the palate,
ultimately balanced.

Vancouver Island

2330 Government St, Victoria, British Colombia, V8T 5G5, **CANADA**
www.vanislandbrewery.com

The inspiration for this company's formation in 1984 was the absence of locally made beers on Vancouver Island. The brewery believes that brewing should be a perfect blend of art and science, with no short cuts.

BREWING SECRET Though the hops and yeast are imported, only the finest Canadian barley is used.

Hermannator
EISBOCK 9.5% ABV
Brewed and then frozen, it is a symphony of complex chestnut colors and spicy flavors.

Hermann's Dark
BAVARIAN LAGER 5.5% ABV
A toasty malt nose with similar flavors on the palate; takes on a somewhat nutty character.

Victory

420 Acorn Lane
Downingtown, PA 19335, **USA**
www.victorybeer.com

Victory Brewing founders Ron Barchet and Bill Covaleski—who met on a school bus in 1973—traveled much of the beer world, apprenticed in Germany, and worked in US micro breweries before starting their own in 1996. The breadth of their interests is reflected in the range of their beers.

BREWING SECRET Victory has long-term contracts with German hop-growers to assure the availability of authentic ingredients for their lagers.

Prima Pils
PILSNER 5.3% ABV
Fresh flowery aromas, cookielike palate, and a solidly bitter-rough finish. Sturdy yet delicate.

Golden Monkey
TRIPLE 9.5% ABV
Spicy, with hints of banana followed by light pepper. Candy-sweet on the palate, with a dry finish.

Wadworth

Devises, Wiltshire,
SN10 1JW **ENGLAND**
www.wadworth.co.uk

Established by Henry Wadworth,
the brewery began producing
beer in 1875 and was expanded
10 years later into an impressive,
red-brick Victorian tower
brewery. The original open
copper is still operational and
wooden casks are used for local
deliveries. A full-time cooper and
a team of dray horses continue
traditional customs.

Wadworth 6X
BEST BITTER 4.3% ABV
A malt and fruit nose, with restrained
hop characteristics developing an
intensity on the palate.

JEB
STRONG BITTER 4.7% ABV
Aromatic wafts of tropical fruit; a rich
malt mouth with some nutty sweetness
on the palate.

Weitra Bräu

Sparkassaplatz 160,
A-3970 Weitra, **AUSTRIA**
www.bierwerkstatt.at

Weitra claims to hold Austria's oldest brewing privilege, issued in 1321. In medieval times, most of the buildings around the town square exercised their right to brew, now there is only one brewpub and this brewery left.

BREWING SECRET This organic specialty brewery, bought by Zwettler in 2002, still brews using open fermenters.

Hadmar
ORGANIC VIENNA LAGER 5.2% ABV
Sweet and malty on the nose and palate; hints of roastyness, bitterness; variable from batch to batch.

Weitra Hell
LAGER 5% ABV
Straw colored, with estery aroma and very little carbonation. Soft on the palate, with a mild hoppyness.

Wells & Young's

Bedford, Bedfordshire,
MK40 4LU **ENGLAND**
www.charleswells.co.uk
www.youngs.co.uk

A major force in British brewing
was created in 2006 from the
partnership of London brewer
Young's and Bedford-based
Charles Wells, two of the most
prodigiously accomplished
operators in the industry. Wells &
Young's cask and bottled ale
portfolio is one of the broadest in
the brewing sector, particularly
after Courage brands—Best Bitter
and Directors Bitter—were added
in 2007 under an agreement with
Scottish & Newcastle.

Wells Bombardier
PREMIUM BITTER 4.3% ABV
Powerful citrus hop aromas meet
malt and dried fruit in a richly
complex medley.

Young's Bitter
BITTER 3.7% ABV
Well-balanced, with citrus hop notes
and enough malt for a flowery and
bready finish.

Westvleteren

Donkerstraat 12,
B8640 Vleteren, **BELGIUM**
www.sintsixtus.be

The Abbey of St. Sixtus of Westvleteren is the reclusive star of the beer world. It sells its beer by telephone reservation only—unwillingly even—as if to emphasize that the operation is run by monks who brew in order to be able to pray, instead of pray in order to sell. Westvleteren voluntarily limits production.

BREWING SECRET This is the only remaining Trappist brewery that still employs solely in-house monks.

Westvleteren Blond
ABBEY ALE 5.8% ABV
A blonde ale that starts with a big grain flavor, followed by very serious hops; best bitterlike.

Westvleteren ABT 12°
ABBEY ALE 10.2% ABV
A truly massive dark Trappist ale: chewy like no other beer, and with a perfect balance between the sweet and bitter notes.

Widmer

929 North Russell
Portland, OR 97227, **USA**
www.widmer.com

More than two decades old, the US-centric Hefeweizen (cloudy but accented by yeast rather than hops) that the Widmer brothers basically invented continues to drive double-digit growth. Widmer and Redhook have merged to form a single company called Craft Breweries Alliance, but Widmer maintains its own brewery.

Hefeweizen

US HEFEWEIZEN **4.9**% ABV
Citrus, particularly lemon zest, is matched against clean, bready-yet-tart wheat. Finale of grapefruit.

Snow Plow

MILK STOUT **5.5**% ABV
Coffee on the nose becomes creamier on the palate, roasted notes blending with rich chocolate.

Williams

Alloa, Clackmannanshire,
FK10 1NT **SCOTLAND**
www.heatherale.co.uk

Alloa was once second only
to Burton upon Trent as a
brewing center, so it is
encouraging to observe
innovative beer styles still
being developed there. Historic
recipes and traditional folklore
methods are skilfully applied.

BREWING SECRET In the Fraoch Ale,
flowering heather is used instead of hops,
reviving an ancient Celtic recipe.

Fraoch Heather Ale
SPECIALITY BITTER **4.1%** ABV
Abundantly floral and aromatic, with
a spicy mint piquancy, malty character,
and whiff of peat.

Kelpie Seaweed Ale
SPECIALITY BITTER **4.4%** ABV
Organic barley from coastal farms and
bladderwrack seaweed in the mash
produce beguiling flavors.

Yanjing

9 Shuanghe Road, Shunyi
District,
Beijing, **CHINA**
www.yanjing.com.cn

The last remaining large
independent brewer in China,
Yanjing often rouses the
attention of the global
brewers. Over the past 25
years Yanjing has developed
into one of the largest beer
producing enterprises in
China. It operates 20 other
breweries on the China
mainland, and its output is
predicted to reach 1.1 billion
gallons (5 million kiloliters)
by 2010.

Yanjing Beer

LAGER 5% ABV

A sweet, golden syrup nose, it has
overlays of biscuits and corn and
pours a sun burst yellow into a glass.
The brewing water is said to be from
unpolluted mineral water deep
under the Yanshan mountain.

Yoho

1119-1 Otai, Saku City,
Nagano 385-0009, **JAPAN**
www.yonasato.com

Yona Yona Ale is perhaps the
most popular craft beer in Japan,
available in brightly colored
cans and on draft all over
Japan. While the recipe predates
head brewer Toshi Ishii (who
previously worked at Stone
Brewing in San Diego), he is
responsible for their second big
success, Tokyo Black, a tasty
porter with remarkable flavor
and smooth balance.

Yona Yona Ale
PALE ALE 5.5% ABV
Square in the American Pale Ale category.
Brisk and citrussy, with Cascade hops
giving a sharp finish.

Tokyo Black
PORTER 5% ABV
This tasty, roasty beer can best be
described as a session porter, with
a unique twist. Brewer Ishii recently
brewed a batch in England.

Yukon Brewing

102A Copper Rd, Whitehorse,
Yukon Y1A 2Z6, **CANADA**
www.yukonbeer.com

Clean water makes clean beer.
Yukon beers start with North
America's cleanest water. Named
by some the Wilderness City,
Whitehorse nestles on the banks
of the famous Yukon River,
surrounded by mountains and
clear mountain lakes. Yukon
makes eight beers, including
one flavored with coffee beans.

Lead Dog Ale

ALE 7% ABV

Intricate malt flavors predominate.
Reminiscent of a porter, it has a slightly
darkened, creamy head.

Discovery Ale

PALE ALE 5% ABV

Brewed using honey made from
Fireweed, the official flower of the Yukon.
It finishes dry on the tongue.

Zagrebacka

Ilica 224, Zagreb, **CROATIA**
www.inbev.com

Zagrebacka Pivovara, Croatia's largest brewer, was established in 1893 and is now owned by InBev. After years of falling beer consumption, the market is now growing again, with domestic lager brands being the most popular segment of the market.

BREWING SECRET Double-malted dark chocolate barley gives the dark lager its prized aromas, flavors, and color.

Ožujsko Pivo
LAGER 5.2% ABV
A golden lager, with a deep, white head. A sweetcorn and malt nose gives way to a fruity finish.

Tomislav Pivo
DARK LAGER 7% ABV
Croatia's strongest beer, this deep ruby-red lager has aromas of roasted malt and coffee, and a dry finish.

Žatec

Žižkovo náměstí 81, 438 01 Žatec,
CZECH REPUBLIC
www.zateckypivovar.cz

There is no escaping it in Czech
beer production—every brewery
uses the town's succulent hops,
and, as far back as 1585, Žatec
beer was praised for "its essence,
strengths, and virtues."

BREWING SECRET Significant recent
investment has upgraded its yeast plant,
restored open fermenters, and introduced
state-of-the-art kegging.

Žatec Blue Label
PREMIUM LAGER **4.6**% ABV
Hints of grassy hop and sweet malt, then
banana with biscuit malt on the palate.

Žatec Export
PILSNER **4.6**% ABV
Bready aroma with herbal notes, some
sweet malt, delicate spicy hop, and
appropriate apple sourness.

Index

This is an index of individual beers only, as the breweries appear in A–Z order in the book.